haven

Also by Chris Madden

haven

FINDING THE KEYS TO
YOUR PERSONAL DECORATING STYLE

By Chris Casson Madden
with Carolyn Schultz

Photographs by Nancy Elizabeth Hill

Clarkson Potter/Publishers
New York

acknowledgments

First of all, I want to thank all of the women (and some men!) who, over the past 15 years, have talked to me about their decorating fears (and triumphs) at countless book signings, store appearances, and decorating seminars. They are the inspiration and the foundation of this book.

And, of course, I wanted to acknowledge my great support team. My husband, Kevin, and my sons, Patrick and Nick, both of whom were very involved in the creation of this book. Thanks, guys! Deb Evans, an extraordinary woman. Thank you! And to Lynn von Kersting, no book is complete without your elegance and panache.

Carolyn Schultz worked 24/7 on this project. Her inspiration and support were invaluable, as was the incredible design vision and talent of Doug Turshen.

Nancy Hill, my fabulous photographer, was again brilliant! And, of course, thanks to the many talents of Barbara Marks!

My office manager, Anthony Ramirez, kept the office running smoothly with Christina Carty's assistance.

I'm indebted, as always, to my great editors at Clarkson Potter, Annetta Hanna and Pam Krauss and Lauren Shakely, for pushing this project to fruition.

Nancy would like to thank William and Montgomery, and Florence Hill, Venetta W., Charles, Jillian, Stephanie, Kate, Gloria and Aldo—you all made it possible. Mark and Cathy, your SUPER E-6; Rick... even still; Chris, your vision, and another chance to work with you and the gang.

Carolyn thanks her family for their love and support—especially Andy, Mia, Claire, Brandon, Ben, Jan, Jonah, Rebecca, Mel, Ruth and friends, Sarah and Laura.

Published by Clarkson Potter/Publishers, New York, New York

Member of the Crown Publishing Group, a division of Random House, Inc.   www.crownpublishing.com

CLARKSON N. POTTER is a trademark and POTTER and colophon are registered trademarks of Random House, Inc.

Printed in Japan

Design by Doug Turshen with Jan H. Greco

Library of Congress
Cataloging-in-Publication Data
is available upon request

ISBN 1-4000-5137-1

10 9 8 7 6 5 4 3 2 1

First Edition

contents

Setting the stage for **romantic** new traditions while commemorating the old—creating comfort, beauty, and satisfaction for loved ones and for self.   19

An appreciation of different cultures and the artifacts and **adventurous** designs gleaned from looking beyond one's own home boundaries.   65

Creating an harmonious, quiet oasis . . . a **serene** home that is relaxing to the body and restorative to the soul.   111

preface

This is a true story. When my husband, Kevin, and I were first married, we received many wedding presents—some right on target, and some unusual! My beloved boss at that time knew about my passion for design and her wedding gift to us was a one-hour session with a top decorator in our new apartment in Manhattan. Serge (happily I don't remember his last name) strolled confidently into our small, but nicely decorated (by me) living room. And for the next hour, he berated, bullied, and insulted us about our design choices. "Oh, that definitely has to go!" he decreed, staring at my husband's college chair from Princeton placed with pride next to our fireplace. And so that long hour went. And from that moment on I learned to trust myself—follow my own design instincts and put aside the decorating fear factor. And in looking back, I can now say that that was a great wedding present (thank you, Lynn) because it steered me toward my true vocation: demystifying, or simplifying, design—for myself and also for others.

I had been to design school, having won a scholarship to the prestigious Fashion Institute of Technology in New York City, and had been focusing more on the design intricacies of apparel than home furnishings. But soon I found myself devouring decorating magazines, falling in love with art history and photography, and being asked by friends to help them decorate their own homes.

After that unforgettable decorating hour, I started to immerse myself in every aspect of home design. I never again wanted to feel so powerless in one of the most important parts of my life— my own home. I wanted to know about concepts—balance, scale, why certain colors made me feel better in a room than other colors, why when I added dimmers to my lights it changed my mood, instantly? So I started taking evening classes in interior design. I went to every showcase house I could and haunted museums and historic homes in New York and throughout the world— the Frick; the restoration rooms at the Met; Cooper-Hewitt; Hildene in Manchester, Vermont;

Versailles in France; and Czar Nicholas II's home in Russia. I gleaned inspiration and deep satisfaction from these visits. I sat in on lectures and seminars and started dragging my husband and young sons to every local antiques show, flea market, or tag sale they would allow me to on weekends.

And I discovered something along the way. While some of us, like the legendary designers Sister Parish and Elsie de Wolfe, are naturally gifted—not "schooled"—in the design arena, almost all of us can learn the basics of home design, and how to apply them, if the tenets of home design are explained and laid out in an easy-to-understand, concrete fashion—even those who consider themselves "decorator-challenged."

Ultimately I recognized that interior and home-furnishings design was quickly becoming my passion (more so than fashion design), and a profession that I wanted to immerse myself in full-time. My first book, *Interior Visions,* became a national best-seller in the design community. I knew then that this was what I wanted to be doing.

So I have continued on that journey—I've been fortunate to be able to talk about decorating and design in so many ways. I have appeared on *Oprah, Today, Good Morning America, CBS Sunday Morning,* and CNN showing you the tricks of the trade; I also had one of the first shows on HGTV (eight years running!); and I write a weekly column on design issues that goes out to more than four hundred newspapers across America. I've spoken at hundreds of decorating seminars, from those held at major department stores, to others at museums, including the Smithsonian and the Chrysler, from small-town bookstores in Winnetka, Illinois, to La Jolla, California, explaining what goes into the design process. I've loved every minute of it—especially the feedback I get from all of you when we get a chance to meet face-to-face. You bring questions, answers, and dilemmas. In other words, it's an incredible exchange of information and energy and yet at the end of each event I hear, "I just want to know how to find my own decorating style." You keep telling me you want the nuts and bolts, the how-to of decorating basics—in an easy-to-understand format.

When I had the great good fortune to appear frequently on her show, Oprah also asked me to devise a system to help her viewers demystify the elements of design . . . to come up with a system that would help women identify their own personal decorating style. And so I did.

What I have found fascinating is that a fear factor crosses the board of design—whether it

be updating your living room, redesigning your bathroom, changing accessories for a seasonal look, or warming up your bedroom. It also cuts across a large strata of our society—from high-powered executives to stay-at-home moms and Generation Xers. You can tell, I've talked to lots of folks out there—maybe even you!—and I know how many still find all this decorating talk intimidating and, at times, overwhelming.

Luckily, times have changed. Many people are beginning to feel more empowered and more confident in their design choices. But I still hear your voices asking me to simplify it, to break it down to the basics, and, most important, to help you find your "look"—your decorating style. Many of you are versed enough in design to say that you prefer a traditional look, or that you're a country person at heart. Others of you say you want something completely contemporary and modern, but you want to use your antiques as well.

I think each one of us gravitates toward a certain look or certain design style, and I've come up with what I consider to be the three most distinct design profiles; I know you fall into one of these: Romantic, someone who feels comfortable with traditional elements in design, but used in a new fresh way; Adventurous, someone who likes to be surrounded by exotic, stimulating interiors; and Serene, someone who gravitates toward calming, neutral spaces.

So, here it is. I hope what you hold now will be your key to unlocking your very own personal, unique style. I will guide you on this journey to turn your home into your haven.

introduction

Our personal tastes come from who we are, our passions and our past experiences, and perhaps where we see ourselves in the future. Some of us gravitate to a particular design style because it's what we grew up with and feel comfortable being around. I recently met a young interior designer, Renee Graham, whose home is a modern gem. Her father was an architect and she feels comfortable living in a contemporary home with spare rooms and clean-line furnishings.

Other design choices can stem from taking the exact opposite approach to one's childhood home. I remember my good friend Mario Buatta—the "Prince of Chintz"—sharing with me his experience of growing up on Staten Island in a very modern house. He took the opposite tack in his life and career, becoming one of the leading proponents of the English country look.

Whatever your influences or your personal preferences are, what really matters is that your home be unified by a combination of decorating basics, whether they are color, pattern, texture, or mood, and that those, when pooled with that much more personal element—your own unique personality—result in not just a corner, or a room, but an entire home you can be happy and content in, one that fits you like a second skin!

What I want to do in this book is to share with you what I think are evocative examples of rooms designed in the new Romantic,

Adventurous, or Serene emotional styles. We'll start by examining the mood or feeling of each room, the elements that make us experience these rooms by enhancing their look, feel, smell, sound, even taste. Then we'll explore the colors you might expect to find in these three different styles, as well as the fabrics, patterns, and textures that help distinguish these rooms. We'll also look at what I like to call the essentials, those specific objects and elements that help define a room's style—the rug, the furniture, the lamp, or the window treatment. You'll see that these essentials *can* come from a wide variety of sources—the things you've inherited, purchased at retail and home decorating shops, found at flea markets or even as curbside treasures.

This book is about turning your home, be it large or small, into your own haven; finding the style that fits who you are; creating a backdrop that makes you feel happy, healthy, creative, stimulated, loved, and loving.

Start with something you love. I always like to say, start with something that grabs you, that you're passionate about, whether it's a piece of furniture you bought while still in college (so many decorators I know say, "the first piece of furniture I ever bought is in this room"), an heirloom rug from a great-aunt, a small figurine whose colors you adore, or the look and mood of a painting that you've always cherished. Start your thought process with something that touches you personally and deeply.

Before you begin trying to find your design style, we should first look at what it is that makes a room work—the "bones" as I call them, that any space needs to make it comfortable and balanced, to "feel right." However,

these are only guidelines that you will need to begin. I hope that the late great designer Billy Baldwin's philosophy of "there are no rules in decorating" will take the intimidation factor out of the decoration equation for you.

THE BONES What is the architecture of the room? Is it clean-lined and spare or more ornate? Does the architecture need beefing up with the addition of molding and detail to make it interesting or do you want to play down the formality of the room? How much natural light does the room receive? Are there good views? Does the out-of-doors offer design inspiration—is it near water, mountains, or a potato field? What is the condition of the floor and the walls? Is there adequate lighting? These are all important questions, and addressing the physical constraints and location inspirations is necessary before you begin to set the mood. With that said, however, consider this: a room spare in architectural details but with ample windows and light may suit a serene space just fine. Some people prefer the look of peeling paint in a gothically romantic room. Adventurous decorators might relish unusual dormers and oddly shaped rooms. Window treatments can help you make allowances for light and view. Floors may just need a simple refinishing, or the addition of wall-to-wall carpeting. Walls may be enhanced by a good paint job or benefit from wallpapering. Some of the rooms you will see in this book address the problems of physical space and how it was dealt with by the homeowner. Just remember, for noncosmetic "fixes," or when the physical features really detract from the mood you wish to create, you may need to consult an architect or a contractor.

LIGHTING The good news about lighting is that it is something that can be fixed with either some good fixtures or the help of an electrician. There are two basic types of lighting you need to think about: task, concentrated lighting that allows you to see what you need to do, and ambient, lighting to set the mood in a room. I believe all rooms need both types of lighting. Lighting determines so many things—it can highlight the colors in your room, the way texture is defined, and even your comfort level. General illumination in a room can be addressed with recessed lights, track lights, hanging fixtures, or wall sconces. When we moved into our new house, the first thing I did was have an electrician install recessed lights in our very dark living room. Since task lighting is essential for reading or doing detailed work —from chopping vegetables to applying mascara—it can be achieved with directed, higher intensity light: a downward reading lamp, undercabinet light fixtures, or a lighted make-up mirror. Ambient lighting can be in the form of recessed high hats, sconces, strings of decorative lights, candles, tea lights, and oil lamps, all of which provide mood. A dimmer switch is an essential element for any electrical light source with a wall switch, but is especially helpful when creating ambient light.

LAYOUT Arranging and rearranging the furniture is one of my favorite decorating "chores" and I'm lucky to have both girlfriends and three strong guys in my life who help me do this! It is the way we get our rooms to work, manage the traffic flow, and establish relationships between our furniture and accessories within the context of a room. The arrangement can be dictated by the physical constraints of a room or to play up a focal point such as a fireplace or picture window. The first thing to do when deciding on an arrangement is to imagine how you want the room to work. For large living rooms or family rooms, for instance, treat the room as if it were several smaller ones, breaking it up into its various activities—a conversation area, a place to play games or have a meal, a special corner for books and reading or a piano or musical instrument. Don't forget computer and TV space.

FOCAL POINT The piece in a room that immediately draws your eye is, in most instances, the focal point. So in each of the rooms in your home, decide what you want that focal point to be—in your bedroom, for instance, it would most likely be your bed. In your living room, perhaps a fireplace or your television set. Some people instead choose an antique armoire or an oversized sofa to be the main attraction in that room.

FLOORING Hardwood plank or parquet; stone such as slate, marble, and granite; composite materials such as terrazzo and concrete; ceramic tile; and mosaic are all "hard" flooring options—durable surfaces that really stand the test of time but may also be hard on the legs in heavy work areas. Laminate and vinyl floors are in between the "hard" and the "soft," such as wall-to-wall carpeting and padded area rugs; because they are cushioned underneath, they make good options for a workplace such as a

kitchen or laundry room. Wall-to-wall carpeting and area rugs are good for **sound protection,** for a more formal element, and where bare feet and baby knees tread. Flooring **considerations** need to be examined before the furniture goes in. And maybe just a sanding and buffing of your existing floor and a well-chosen area rug are all that are necessary.

FLOW I've come to the conclusion that many of us do have a predominant style that we are drawn to again and again and one that makes us feel great, but that doesn't mean all our rooms have to be decorated in that same style. Your style might express itself differently in your living room than in your bedroom, for example. Perhaps you're like me and want a calmer, more serene bedroom to relax in, but really need an invigoratingly adventurous living room for entertaining guests. What's important when decorating rooms in different styles is to have something that **unifies** the spaces within a sight line—when you can see from the kitchen, through the

dining room, to the study, for instance. A carpet that runs from one room to the next, a color that is picked up in either a pattern or a solid, or a texture that unifies the space, such as a grass cloth wallpaper or sisal carpet, helps make that transition calmly from one room to another—instead of suggesting a showcase house.

FURNITURE Like the other removable objects in your home, furniture can be what you've inherited, purchased at a retail store, or found in an antiques store, flea market, or as a "curbside" treasure. Your first purchase or find should address the basic comforts—having places to sleep, sit, and dine. After that, furniture can be the unexpected—pieces used in ways other than how they were originally intended. Or they can be unusual and **unique pieces** that strike your fancy. We have completely moved away from having matching sets in our homes these days—eclectic furnishings are very much in style.

Romantic	Adventurous	Serene

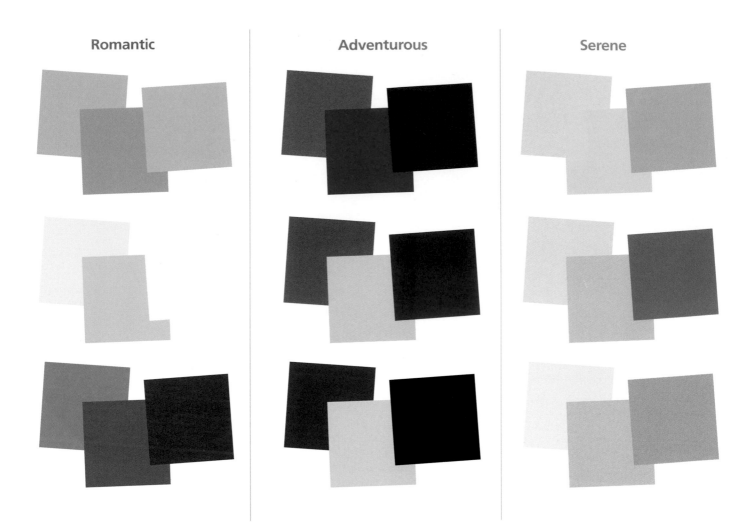

COLOR Our passion for color, or sometimes the lack of it, and the way we use color with pattern can be one of the most important design choices because it really does help determine the mood and atmosphere of a room, making it feel instantly calm or vibrant, quiet or stimulating, cool or warm. What colors are in your closet? Do you prefer sunny, warm reds and yellows or do you favor the coolness of icy blues and greens?

Monochromatically colored spaces that use one hue and include softer tints and deeper tones of that same color can feel very soothing and calming, but unless they are broken up by rich and varied texture—the visual and tactile contrast of matte and shiny, silky or rough—they can be dull and lifeless. To help you understand some of the color terms I use in the book and

the relationship of colors to each other, here is a color chart and key definitions.

Color schemes help establish the mood and emotion of a room through the effective use and balance of color.

Primary Colors: red, yellow, blue.

Neutral Colors: colors that contain little color saturation (white through gray through black).

Complementary Colors: colors opposite one another on the color wheel.

Romantic: related or analogous color scheme, colors that are close together on the color wheel.

Adventurous: contrasting color scheme, a contrast of different weights and complements with the punch of primary color for emphasis.

Serene: monochromatic color scheme, shades, tints, and tones of one color.

PATTERN Like color, the patterns we select for inclusion in our rooms help determine not only the mood and atmosphere but also a theme or an idea. Pattern is the repeat of an object or design element—elephants, flowers, vertical stripes, dots—and the repetition, the amount of that pattern, speaks volumes. In a serene space, pattern may be textural only—the grid design from the loose weave of a natural fiber or the nubby repeat of a knitted throw. Romantic and adventurous tend to explore many different patterns, and the play of these patterns —the mix of florals and checks, animal prints and ticking stripes, for example—gives the room vitality and interest.

TEXTURE Texture is a key element for bringing vitality to our homes, but it can be difficult to understand because it is something that

involves both sight and touch. We look at texture and first see its surface, rough or smooth, and we know what it feels like before we actually touch it. Don't stop with fabrics. You can bring textural excitement into your spaces via walls, floors, or your focal point—a painting, the fireplace mantel, or the view out your window. Sometimes texture is necessary to help bring definition to a room; in brightly colored spaces where prints and patterns are the dominating design element, textural differences are important for visual clarity. For instance, a room covered in smooth cotton two-toned toile or a multicolored floral chintz needs the balance of a rougher texture—a wool or sisal rug, wood bed posts, or the mottled surface of an antique mirror. Corduroy fabrics, loopy rugs, even lace curtains are all about texture—these are elements that make us want to just reach out and touch.

ACCESSORIES Your personal interests and passions are expressed through your accessories—these objects, artworks, books, and mementos are the treasures that make your room special and uniquely you. Just remember that your collected treasures or your material possessions should never become just stuff to fill the room. They should speak to you—you know the feeling when you have to have something or can't let something go. Since most of us are born collectors, anyway, try to contain your treasures by arranging, editing, and grouping these items by common threads or by themes—color, shape, material—and positioning them on a shelf to help keep clutter at bay. Even if your philosophy is "more is more," balance these "objets" with something more spare in the room—minimal window treatments, white walls, or bare floors. As you look at the rooms in these pages, you will see some fabulous and creative ideas for hanging pictures, grouping your accessories to create vignettes, using decorative pillows and throws for punch, and using special "finds" in unusual ways to bring out the best in your home's interiors.

Identifying Your Design Preference

1. What is in your closet, which phrase best describes your wardrobe?
A. Very tailored, black, brown, tan or gray suits, slacks, and skirts with lots of white shirts and piles of neutral-colored sweaters—cashmere, cotton, and wool.
B. A bit trendy with a mix of different fabrics—herringbones, tweeds, lace and solid colors and patterns—plaid, stripes, and florals mixed with solid and patterned sweaters and lots of accessories.
C. Casual and relaxed, with a great mix of different fabrics, styles, and designers, denims, handmade sweaters and accessories.

2. How do you like to entertain or be entertained at home?
A. An elegant cocktail party with fine wine, stylish hors d'oeuvres, and great martinis.
B. Sit-down dinners pulling out all the stops—multi-course meals using your best things—candelabra, china, crystal, and silver.
C. A buffet or pot luck with lots of guests, people bringing their favorite or signature dishes, sitting around comfortably on furniture and floor cushions, oversized linen napkins on laps.

3. Your dream house would be?
A. A mid-century modern gem.
B. A rambling Victorian with a wrap-around porch.
C. An old stone, former carriage house.

4. What group of goods would you be most inclined to look for at a flea market or antiques store?
A. Russell Wright dinnerware, a mid-century modern chair, a book showcasing black-and-white photography or architecture.
B. An old trophy cup, a vintage printed tablecloth, fabric- or wall-paper-covered boxes, etched champagne flutes, a Bentwood coat rack.
C. A shed moose antler, old Persian carpet pieces, a vintage metal postcard rack with or without postcards, an old vintner's basket.

5. Which fabrics or textile group would you most likely include in your bedroom?
A. White, tan or gray cotton sheets, soft wool blanket.
B. Floral, stripes or colorful sheets with a toile, chenille or brightly

BALANCE Romantic. . . Adventurous. . . Serene. . . no matter what your personal design style, remember—one of the keys—there must be a balance within the walls of your home. The balance in this case is not just about symmetry or proportion, although they do make a difference. If you have a large or heavy piece on one side of your living room, you don't want the other side of the room to feel as if it can lift off or "float away," so you'd put an equally heavy object there such as a large armoire on one end and a sofa on the other side. It doesn't have to be the same shape; it's just that the visual weight should balance. Balance—when it comes to mood—is also about editing and arranging, maintaining a good traffic flow, and making sure rooms are as comfortable and soothing as you want them to be. Balance has to do with color and pattern, as well—the proportion of one color to another. For example, if you use primary colors in a room, you don't want to give equal weight to all of them or it will look like a circus. A blue room might demand a touch of red or a spark of yellow. Balance is also about point and counterpoint, balancing the visual weight and the visually perceived texture—light and dark, hard and soft, well worn and shiny, lightweight and heavy. Balance in the new American home is about getting all the elements right, everything we just discussed—a starting piece, lighting, layout, a focal point, flooring, flow, furniture, color, pattern, and texture. Which brings me to the last consideration—that icing on the cake that really makes the room come together, the sensory elements.

covered down duvet.
C. Ticking stripe or neutral flannel sheets with Pendleton blankets, down comforter, old quilts.

6. Which vignette or display would you find the most pleasing to your eye?
A. A grouping of three cream-colored pottery pieces on an open shelf.
B. A tray filled with vintage cups and saucers, silver spoons and a stack of majolica plates.
C. A bookshelf filled with old volumes, an antique spice box from India, and a small oil painting of an Italian villa.

7. Which piece of furniture would you be inclined to buy before another?

A. A modern, clean-lined metal and wood bench.
B. An upholstered settee from a tag sale.
C. A kilim-upholstered storage/coffee table.

8. Which rug might you consider for your dining room?
A. A sisal area rug.
B. An Aubusson floral rug.
C. An Oriental area rug.

9. Which statement best fits you when describing window treatments?
A. I don't really care for window treatments but would consider a linen panel or wooden blinds.
B. I love lush and colorful silk drapes with lots of dressmaker detail.
C. I would be inclined to use

bamboo shades and create a valance using paisley fabrics or vintage textiles.

10. Your idea of a great vacation would be?
A. A spa retreat in the desert.
B. A resort hotel on a tropical beach.
C. White-water rafting in the rain forests of Costa Rica.

11. Which chair would you prefer?
A. A Shaker rocker.
B. A down-filled, upholstered slipper chair.
C. A kilim-covered wing chair.

Mostly A's—Serene
Mostly B's—Romantic
Mostly C's—Adventurous

the sensory elements of Sight, Sound,

Scent, Touch, and Taste are what make our homes our personal havens. In these fast-paced times that we live in, we need our homes to be comfort zones, antidotes to the sometimes frenetic outside world of work, school, the gym, the grocery store, or the shopping mall. This calming ambience or mood can begin to set the tone of your design style from the moment you first walk in. It is why the music you listen to, the tastes and smells of cooking, the fragrances of your candles and room scents, the way the lights are dimmed or the candles are lit, the monochromatic or complementary colors used, and the textural essences are so important. The sensory elements are crucial in how you set the mood and make your home comfortable and pleasurable for you and the people in your life.

SIGHT Present rooms with a view. Pleasing furniture layouts, thoughtful vignettes, interesting collections, books, architectural artifacts, great wallpaper, and paint and items of personal importance.

SOUND Select music options to fit all moods—jazz, swing, classical, vocal, pop, folk, soundtrack—it's your preference! Turntable and vinyl records, CDs or tapes and a player. Fountains, white noise machines, chimes, sounds that are stimulating or soothing.

SCENT Invest in scented candles, potpourris, scented sachets, and room sprays, or simply let the smells from a floral bouquet infuse your rooms with delightful aroma.

TOUCH Make a room come alive! Furnish your rooms with rich and varied textures—soft, smooth, or bristly textures underfoot; natural upholstery materials that allow skin to breathe; nubby textures such as linen or chenille; velvety textures such as faux fur; velvet cottons or silks

in decorative pillows and throws. Choose textures that look as good as they feel.

TASTE Indulge in a stylish candy dish, an inviting bar setup, or a well-stocked larder full of fun foods for entertaining—nuts, crackers, cheeses, olives, oils, breadsticks, wines, liquors, flavored waters, and aperitifs. Placing trays around the house makes it okay to indulge in taste sensations in any room.

I believe that the design of a home is an organic process—it's about adapting to meet our changing needs, building, layering, and adding new discoveries, editing others. Some essential and easy ways to keep our homes alive, exciting, and always inviting involve playing with those sensual elements we just discussed—sight, sound, scent, taste, and touch—perhaps adjusting the mood, color, or texture. For instance, think of how you feel and what a difference it makes when you receive a gift of fresh flowers and put them in a room. Not only will you be uplifted, but the room will be as well!

Each and every time you walk
into a room, it should appeal to

your five senses.

romantic

romantic mood

I'm sure you've all had this experience: you're in a crowd of people—either at a movie, a wedding, or during a Fourth of July town celebration—when everyone in the crowd, inspired by some occurrence or spectacle, sighs a collective, **"Aaahh!"** When I'm giving one of my decorating seminars, this invariably happens when I show a particular slide from one of my books illustrating a young girl's room, the bed and windows draped with a lusciously soft, green-and-white hydrangea cotton print. Sunlight spilling into the room casts a glow over a crystal bowl of fresh-cut roses. The "aaahh" is audible. Romantic. You know it when you see it, you respond when you feel it.

Romantic feelings can jolt us, eliciting feelings of longing and desire when we least expect them. Romantic is, of course, more than just the hope or expression of love between two people. Romantic is conjuring a time, place, and feeling and then incorporating that memory or fantasy into the mood you create in your home—re-creating the memory of fresh-picked summer blueberries on a beautiful summer day.

When I want to invoke romance, I think of trips to visit my younger sister, Jeannie, in France, her adoptive homeland. With her family I share the ritual of the long, leisurely Sunday afternoons spent dining, sipping wine, sharing stories in their old stone dining room. I also enjoy the sensual stimulation of the French countryside and the emotions that accompany coming upon an entire field of lavender, a table laden with warm croissants, fresh berry jam and steaming bowls of café au lait, or hearing a song full of hope and yearning even when I don't understand all the words.

A Romantic style in decorating can be rich with deep sensory overtones and drama or have a newer tone, which is subtler, based on promise, fresh with possibility, and bright with color.

Luxurious appointments such as an antique table, china, crystal, and old silver pieces may be some of the elements of the romantic mood but so, too, are a vintage distressed painted dresser found at a flea market, Chinese paper lanterns, or a chaise lounge slipcovered in a soft white terry cloth. Romantic style finds expression also in lush, fresh, and abundant interiors, alluding to new possibilities, unexplored territory, and hopes for a shining future.

Simple or grand, luxurious or rustic, the romantic mood is expressed with feeling and exuberance for life. And let's not forget the five senses—music, fresh tastes, and comfort items—pillows, soft fabrics, flowers, and luscious scents—all are presented generously.

Romantic style captures a time, place, or feeling. It can be rich with deep sensory overtones—the smell of a bouquet, the feel of a fabric—or more subtle, based on promise, fresh with possibility and bright with color, evoking a bike ride on a summer's day, the basket full of flowers.

Each of these objects, whether grouped together or on its own, helps create a romantic mood by capturing through color, shape, and form items cherished not only for their feel in the hand but also for the way they touch the heart of the collector. Smoothed and polished horn cups, 19th-century majolica, weathered shells, urns, natural objects—glass and stoneware—and picturesque vignettes, combined with the flourish of floral bouquets, help enhance an appreciation for the garden and a palette's worth of vibrant color in these evocatively romantic images.

romantic texture

Romantic rooms are like a living scrapbook of memories and experience, and the textures in these spaces should reflect a life lived to the fullest. Romantic textures are the bits and pieces that add up to a vital whole—the photographs, sea glass, books, inherited furniture, wedding silver, trophy cups, fresh, bright linens mixed with vintage fabrics, and flea market pottery.

Romantic textures are abundant and varied. They have been aged by time to a fine patina like the pages of old books and worn, painted surfaces. They feel good against the skin, like woolen knits, cashmere and mohair throws and blankets, or the crisp feel of a cool patterned cotton or linen. Abundance is expressed in textures that have been layered—throws on the backs of sofas, pillows on dining chairs, silk rugs layered over sisal or a cotton summer slipcover layered over a heavier winter weave on an easy chair.

They have heft and substance in the hand like a cut-crystal bowl, a hand-blown hurricane shade, or a dessert spoon of sterling silver. They enhance the light like gauzy sheers at the window or a warm colored lampshade that casts a rosy glow.

The new Romantic style references history and tradition and attempts to create the idyllic. Flowers are an important part of this charm and whimsy. These natural elements also express texture—think of flowers such as freesia, snapdragons, white roses, Queen Anne's lace.

Romantic is generous and often adheres to a "more is more" philosophy—more fabric, more flowers, cushions, and billowy comfort. Romantics gather and hold dear objects that inspire reminiscences while letting flowers, ample textures, and the tactile sensation of soft and supple materials convey their generous impulses.

Romantic styling emphasizes the importance of decorating as an expression of love and comfort—for family, friends, and, most important, as a purely indulgent gift to yourself. As such, romantic rooms can be public or intimate spaces. Bedrooms, for obvious reasons, lend themselves to the romantic touch and a bed is the perfect platform for a display of different textures and colors.

Bathrooms and dressing rooms where personal pampering is encouraged are great places to stack soft terry cloth towels in a basket, use that old silver tray for soaps, or display a collection of fragrance bottles. The dining room also resonates to the romantic because it is a public space where conversation can become intimate over the sharing of food and drink.

romantic color & pattern

Romantic colors, for me, can be found at a farmer's market in Vermont, on the doors of the houses in Nantucket, in the jockeys' silks at the Saratoga racetrack in August, or in the sherbet colors of beach towels against the ocean sand. Take your color keys for this style from the places and images that excite your imagination and make you feel like anything is possible.

Both hot and cool colors are in this palette—the pinks, oranges, and yellows of summer's bounty and bouquets as well as the blues, greens, and violets of the ocean. A fresh, inviting color scheme that I have found works well with romantic styling is using related color, that is, colors that lie close together on the color spectrum. If you imagine a color "splayed," or presented as a series, you recognize the relationship of pink, red, and orange in the hot hues or violet, blues, and greens on the cooler side.

A monochromatic scheme works in the romantic style as well, especially when you use a more vibrant color than the expected white or creamy hue. Here you can let your imagination go, saturating a room with lime, chartreuse, or a pink coral in all their various shades.

I find it easier to select fabrics for a romantic style by starting with a pattern that appeals to me emotionally—perhaps the greens, pinks, and yellows of an English floral chintz, or the contrasting combination of a cheerful blue-and-white gingham with abstract patterned pillows.

Florals are the most obvious, and perhaps feminine, expressions of the Romantic style. They might be overlaid on a striped background, or tea-stained for a vintage look. They can be seen in small, colorful bouquets, in large, graphic displays on a vivid field, or as a singular bloom against a snowy white weave.

Crewel fabrics can be great accent pieces for pillows or bed shams, or a wonderful choice for an upholstered chair. These stitched patterns are loosely embroidered with twisted yarn on a linen or cotton cloth. Appliqué done with beads, embroidery, or bits of fabrics are very popular as vintage collectibles. *Matelasse* come in almost as many patterns as there are snowflakes and work well in pulling together many patterns.

Other nonfloral choices for the romantic are large or small gingham prints, toiles in two or three color schemes, stripes with bold, bright awning appeal, or the vintage look of old pillow or mattress ticking. Any or all of these fabrics can be embellished with embroidery, beads, appliqué, or fringe, giving them a fresh charm, movement, and even sound.

Proximity to the sea imbues this room with an

inherently romantic quality of light.

This room is defined by its relationship to the water—the sparkling blue waters of the Long Island Sound are a stone's throw from the French doors and the glass wall that separate the house from the garden. This proximity imbues the room with the unique quality of light reflected from a sea's mirrored surface.

Understated glamour is key to this romantic look—from the dark, slender graceful lines of the furniture to the light, neutral-toned but highly textured linens, cottons, and glazed silks that cover them. The art resonates elegance, with the stark black-and-white beauty of Picasso's women framed on the wall.

The white walls in this room are tinted with blue—evoking the shoreline setting as does the intimate seating area with the vibrant blues in the rug. Other colors are determined by sand and sky—the checked fabric on the sofa and the blues in the Persian rug.

Textural elements here, like a true romantic's, are smooth and reflective—the antique horn cups on the low glass table, the silver and crystal on the bar, the shiny leaves of the orchid juxtaposed against the 19th-century glass, porcelain, and books on the rosewood table—all romantic collectibles.

How to get this look

0→ Emphasize the contrast of light and dark with light upholstery and curtains against dark floors and furniture, dark lamps against white walls, and by hanging black-and-white photography or other works of art in similarly colored frames and mats.

0→ Keep your window treatments to a minimum; opt for balloon shades rather than more formal drapes.

0→ Choose furniture with curved, almost sculptural lines.

ives of LEE MILLER ANTONY PENROSE

YLE BY SALADINO

The Grand Book of French Style DEMACHY and BAUDOT

MANET

Matisse Portraits

Museum and Its Collections

A gilt-framed inspiration board is the visual focal point in the generously sized office of an Atlanta designer and entrepreneur. A collection of photographs, fabrics, magazine tear sheets, and invitations stand out from a backdrop of staff and notes—irregularly spaced pages of sheet music that paper the board. A library of books is stacked invitingly underneath, alternately providing additional bits of inspiration and pedestals on which to display architectural remnants, wire sculpture, paintings, and plants. The walls are a neutral white, causing the touches of gilt in the frame, lampshade, chair, and hardware to "pop." A honey-colored sisal carpet marries the accents of gold with the warm tones of the door and woodwork. Reflective surfaces—the glass of the table and the silver cup—provide textural contrast with the sisal, wood, and upholstered seating while a round medallion and side table and the curvy lamp and wire sculpture break up the geometric squares and rectangles. This designer's skilled and intuitive use of textures and decorative elements makes her workplace a setting in which creativity rules.

Designer Ingrid Leess's style is fresh, original, and relaxed. She has a great eye for color and composition, honed from an early age by watching her mother haunt tag sales and auctions. "She was a great recycler," says Leess. "The oil painting is from her. In fact, most of my furniture was bought secondhand—I only buy new fabrics and a few new accessories. The mix is the best way to get a unique, personal, undecorated look."

Ingrid claimed the colors of the ocean beach—the dunes, sand, shells, and water—for her family room. She uses white on walls, the sofa, and tables throughout the room, to let those colors stand out. The hues of blues and greens are cool and relaxing. When using a related color scheme, it is interesting to use many different shades of blues and greens, exploring the tonal variations as Leess has done here, rather than just the two basic colors. And, although Leess is a romantic, she shies away from florals, preferring checks, plaids, and stripes for textural interest.

The black table, a recent find, pleases her eye since it adds, in her words, "an exclamation point."

"I get my color inspiration from the shore… it is my favorite place to be."

In a turn-of-the-century home in Annapolis, Maryland, Eleanor Niermann has created a fresh romantic look by mixing new furniture pieces that look classically old with authentic antiques for a look that is young and modern in appeal. She does this by arranging her furnishings against a spare white background to emphasize light and space. Her father's company, Niermann Weeks, designed the sofa, ottoman, armchair, and the round side table, all which have antiqued and patinated surfaces to blend effortlessly with the other pieces she has collected. A Persian carpet, a bouquet of pink lilies, touches of gold on the sofa, and a contented pet all add the elements of romance. At the window, the light and view are softened with a geometric wooden screen, a copy of an antique zinc screen from her father's firm. Old wood plank floors have been stripped and left unstained, in keeping with the soft, neutral background. The large painting over the sofa is a piece of "found" art; the accidental masterpiece was once the top of a studio work surface.

A fresh mix of **classically proportioned** furniture and subtle neutral tones imbues this living room with a romantic appeal.

In the living room,

Eleanor Niermann propped a distressed mirror over a marble-topped antique console. The details on the mirror, from the weathered silvery surface to the burnished brass medallion top, convincingly belie its age, making it appear centuries older than the authentic console. Throughout the room, old leather or papered trunks add texture and age with their nailhead trim, peeling surfaces, or antiqued hardware.
BELOW: A Japanese screen creates a strong design element. A raffia-covered chair adds natural texture.
RIGHT: An armchair and an antique faux-bamboo brass floor lamp are set against the scenic backdrop of a circa 1800 wallpaper screen.

How to get this look

0—ᴛ Mix old and new—dare to place disparate styles and periods in the same room. Or, emphasize an antique piece by juxtaposing it with modern shapes and materials such as a contemporary painting in a classically appointed room.

0—ᴛ Add color and texture with one important piece of wall art such as the wallpaper screen.

0—ᴛ Use reproductions of classic objects and shapes to stay within your decorating budget.

Make sure that the objects we use every day give **satisfaction.**

"I tend to be rather tailored in my approach," confesses the owner and designer of this graceful dining room, "but I absolutely fell in love with this fabulous silk and felt the drapes could make the room. The ruffles are a bit of a flourish, but they make the curtains feel more romantic." The room is subtle, complementary to the architectural details, but not without its quirky touches. Naturalistic egg plates from Tiffany & Co. are displayed on a 19th-century Irish mahogany console while a mercury lamp adds soft luster to this still life. On the mantel, a collection of porcelain fruit and vegetables is a contemporary version of 18th-century originals. The worn leather chairs with their "found" finish patina were discovered in a barn in Normandy, where they had been stored for more than a hundred years. They flank a highly polished English mahogany table. The Patrick Henry Bruce painting with its soft colors and simple composition sets the tone for this romantically elegant yet restrained dining room.

This room is composed of carefully

edited elements that

complement the classic architectural details.

The wallpaper is original to the house, a Gracie paper, hand-painted in China and more than fifty years old. It establishes the color tone with its strokes of luscious cream flowers on a celadon field. Subtle touches of gold add a luminescent quality—it appears to glow, in sunlight and candlelight. "I tried to replace it, but in doing so I realized that I couldn't find anything more lovely than the patina and softening this paper has acquired over the years," says Toni.

English and French porcelain— another of Toni's passions—convey elegance and restraint. On the mantel, a pair of 19th-century English hurricane lamps flank hand-painted French plates. The corner display nook is also restrained, with three plates and a covered compote.

A French Aubusson rug covers a dark-stained, wide-plank floor. Wainscoting meets the wallpaper at chair-rail height. The set dressing is perfect. The look is quietly romantic, ready for the evening to unfold.

Toni Gallagher imagined this room for her family and friends. Like a set designer, she created a stage on which the drama of her dinner parties can unfold. It is unabashedly romantic, more English than in England. "The American take on English design usually looks a bit more 'done,'" explains Toni. "We can't help it. The look is not organic here, we have to re-create it and in doing so, we probably embellish."

The table and chairs are 19th-century English, as are the candlesticks and centerpiece bowl. The crystal and silver on the sideboard include pieces inherited from both her maternal and paternal grandparents as well as objects she has collected in her travels. "Candlesticks are my passion," says Toni. "They really set the mood."

"Dining rooms are about the people and the romantic setting you want to create for them."

A few well-placed splashes of blue and green—in glass on the sideboard, in a throw on the back of the settee, in the weathered hue of an old porch balustrade, now a lamp, and in the soft color of a topiary and flowers—enliven a simple, monochromatic color palette of browns, tans, creams, and whites.

The room is small and the details were few. To add architectural elements—a necessary ingredient in a romantic room—"do-it-yourselfer" Ingrid Leess added inexpensive details by painting faux picture moldings and adding a chair rail using a ¼-inch-deep stock molding glued to the walls.

A mélange of hand-me-downs attracts the eye, including a mirror she inherited from her mother casually placed in a corner of the dining room, "the only place it would fit in the house." The accidental placement adds drama and dimension, increasing the size of the room. It has also become a key romantic element for intimate dinner parties. She added a pickled-oak top to give new life to a damaged table, and as a finishing touch, inexpensive Swedish-style chairs were recovered in an embroidered crewel fabric.

"The candlelight from the chandelier is reflected and moves around the room . . . it is magical."

Our guest bedroom with its four-poster twin beds was inspired by a stay in a romantic Connecticut inn. I haven't changed this space much since I found the cream-and-white wallpaper and wonderful coral-patterned fabric ten years ago.

Guests are treated to fresh bouquets and all the amenities we can muster, including a collection of the latest books, a water carafe, and plenty of pillows.

I recently redecorated the room opposite. The strong red-and-white toile wallpaper, normally used in larger spaces, creates an instant intimacy. Using the same pattern in the window visually expands the space and adds a romantic element of texture. Built-ins hold boxes, books, and on a petite circular cabinet sits a vintage bronze urn, perfect for my spring tulips.

How to get this look

0—⊤ Find a fabric you love and indulge! Use it for bed comforters and curtains. Find a wallpaper in a soft stripe. It will add color and texture.

0—⊤ Select a toile-pattern wallpaper and keep it fresh with lots of white contrast—in woodwork, carpet, and upholstery.

0—⊤ The gilt and black circular mirror is deliberately oversized and makes the small room appear larger.

"I didn't start out to create a romantic bedroom, but I guess that is just how I see things," explains designer Toni Gallagher of her master suite. "I respond to colors that are soft and glowing, wood that is warm with patina—and flowers. I love my garden, especially the roses. These are elements I always try and bring into the rooms I create."

Rich English country fabrics were the inspiration for this master suite. "I love the muted combination of celadon and cream with the more vibrant touch of pink." A simple green-and-white silk stripe for the dressing table, drapes, and lining in the bed canopy play off the more patterned florals.

The background for this bedroom is understated and calm with the same color palette—cool celadon walls, a pale green Wilton carpet, and a damask-cream covered chaise. The theme of florals is also echoed in the framed botanical prints, the porcelain plates, and the painted metal chandelier.

How to get this look

O—▸ Be generous with your fabrics—windows, bedding—adding dressmaker details to truly make it feminine.

O—▸ Collect ornate silver frames for your family snapshots and portraits.

O—▸ To soften the lighting, select silk or fabric-covered lampshades.

Something as simple as the introduction of a new pattern can mean the difference in mood—changing what was a peaceful, calm ambience into a decidedly more lively and playful space. A classic Marimekko fabric fashioned into a duvet was the catalyst for this reaction in the once austere bedroom of eighteen-year-old Julia Turshen. "You could definitely say I'm a minimalist," says Turshen of her style. "I am drawn to clean lines and no clutter." But when she got the duvet cover as a gift, she was pleased with how it changed her room. "I've always been a big Marimekko fan. It's fun! I love the big pattern and how it plays off the white walls."

This vibrant display of color seems to float on the low platform bed. The backdrop of the unadorned windows, the oversized paper lantern, and the subtly painted-out trim emphasize the color punch and Turshen's preference for the understated. Red-and-white striped floor cushions, a red bench, and a red Knoll chair provide visual counterpoints in the room.

In this old house, the look becomes fresh and young with the use of glossy, reflective paint, spare accessories, and the play of pulsating color.

A contemporary space in a Greek Revival house— a romantic splash of color brings it to life.

Blue-and-white gingham
bed drapes
add a light, luscious air of romance.

A lyrical photograph provided the inspiration for the romantic look in this bedroom. The image that excited Ingrid Leess's imagination was an old estate room bed, blue-and-white checked drapes framing the cornice. "I fell in love with the contrast of the aged patina with the crisp fabric," explains Leess. "I knew I wanted to re-create that feel."

Leess ingeniously duplicated the mood of that photo without the expense of a European estate bed or antique textiles. Old painted house shutters behind the bed and simple crown molding, mitered and attached to the ceiling joists, add shape, texture, color and patina.

To finish off the look, Leess added pattern and texture with a collection of vintage and new printed and embroidered pillows. Fresh flowers, tag sale oil paintings, a simple reading light, and a comfortable chair were the only elements needed to complete this evocative picture of romance.

This romantic bedroom with its handcrafted four-poster bed and night tables and its layered creamy white linens is a bow to Shaker simplicity kicked up a notch by the self-assured hand of interior designer Tinatin Kilaberidze. An antique Persian rug, its hues mellowed over the years, provides the jumping-off point for color—a gentle lavender on the walls, the blue and white of a generously pleated bed skirt, and the brilliant green of the surrounding garden. Diaphanous linen curtains encircle the room, changing the walls from panels of translucent light to windows that frame the incredible scenery of the Vermont mountains. They are simply hooked on wire cable, letting them slide with ease. A gauzy sheer panel of the same linen is draped over the bed canopy, embellished with a hand-tied rose knot.

"Our house is a marriage of ideas, totally collaborative," says Rochelle Udell, speaking of the home she shares with her husband, Doug Turshen. Sympathetic to their circa 1840 Greek Revival house's roots, both creative directors have produced an architecturally rich yet open and airy gathering place, large enough for their family of four aspiring chefs. This newly renovated kitchen reflects a variety of periods and styles. The coffered ceiling, garden-trellis light fixtures, glass-fronted cabinets, and marble-topped island capture the look of an English manor kitchen. The trestle table, rush chairs, and painted cupboards have French country appeal, while the vinyl checked floor, red banquette, and vintage diner signs are purely American mid-century. The combined effect is friendly and happy, a perfect place to savor the love of cooking and eating, and their favorite place for hanging out together as a family.

romantic essentials

The Romantic style implies comfort—deep cushions, soft fabrics, plush carpet—and those with romantic sensibilities know that comfort lies in these essentials. Let's take a closer look at these elements.

In the romantic room upholstered furniture is **curvy,** overscaled, and sink-into-able. Or, it is classically proportioned and styled but reupholstered in a fresh new way—an understated Louis XV chair paired with the intensity of a Marimekko print or a nubby linen.

Slipcovers can make romantic furniture look like it's wearing a tailored or loose-fitting garment. **Dressmaker details**—exposed buttons; flanged, ruffled, or mitered edges; baffled or tufted cushion tops—make this look finished. Loose-fitting slipcovers lend a more carefree, unstructured air.

Wicker or painted furniture, in whites, blacks, primary colors, or soft pastels, provides color and texture in a room.

Curtains should be allowed to move, to break into a room when they catch a breeze, whether luxurious lengths of glazed cotton, velvet, heavy linen or silk, topped with swags, overlays, and contrasting fabrics and patterns, or sheers of handkerchief linen, silk, organdy, or a delicate nylon. Hardware can be **embellished** with scrolls or fleurs-des-lis. Unexpected curtain rods can be fashioned from an old towel holder or a stretched piece of string or wire.

Lighting is important in every room and especially so here to create the soft, **uncomplicated** level that romantics appreciate. Lamps should be shapely—turned wood, simple glass forms, urns, curvy jars, and vases. Lampshades should follow suit in beautiful fabrics and colors.

Romantic floors can be neutral or more noticeable, bare or covered. Sisal provides a neutral backdrop either as a wall-to-wall covering or an area rug. You can layer rugs over sisal for a richer, warmer look. Antique rugs such as faded Persians or Aubussons can complement the patina of an older hardwood or planked floor. Or, look for simple woven rugs such as cotton runners with a colorful stripe or vintage rag rugs. Floral needlepoint or handpulled tufted area rugs and printed flat wool wall-to-wall carpets are also good choices.

Candles and their accoutrements—the holders, candelabra, wooden trays, or a collection of mismatched candlesticks you've gathered from Grandmother and tag sales—are important accessories the romantic can't live without. Add reflective surfaces such as glass shapes and mirrors, old oil portraits, frames, or furniture with a touch of gold or gilt.

Walls provide a background for your rooms. Think of them as places to display texture by adding molding and **architectural details** if they are lacking, or play up the advantages of beaded board or the rustic charm of stone or brick. Adding detail can be inexpensive and as simple as applying a fresh new pattern of wallpaper.

The important thing in gathering your romantic treasures and searching for the essentials is the pure delight you find in these objects, the story they tell, or the memory they evoke.

Lucy and Scout, lucky Beagles in the home of Turshen and Udell, eat from retro-style dog dishes on a gray-and-white checkerboard grid linoleum floor.

Chinoiserie red toile wallpaper with matching fabric shade adds depth, texture, and interest to the walls and windows in my small personal space in our former home in Westchester, New York.

An urn-shaped glass lamp with a simple white linen shade is romantic in form and in the way it casts a voluptuous glow.

Key essentials of the Romantic Décor—curvy shapes,

An elegant slipper chair is freshly dressed and transformed with a tailored blue-and-white toile and gingham slip-cover. Dressmaker details—the inverted pleat, contrasting welt, and back pillow—add the romantic touch.

Ruffled, scalloped edges, multiple shades of celadon and green, and a thin ceramic profile make this tableware romantic and appropriate for wall, mantel, and table-top display.

Twin beds, dressed alike in blue-and-white sheets, mix both narrow and wide stripes with floral coverlets on antique iron bed frames against a beaded board wall. A mid-century modern lamp adds a hip note to the nostalgic setting.

Glass-fronted cabinets in the Turshen/Udell kitchen house an extensive array of variously shaped but tonal ceramics and stoneware—collectible cake stands, pitchers, mixing bowls, plates, and mortars and pestles.

Bolts of cashmere from India in romantic hues of celadon, coral, pink, lavender, and fuchsia.

luscious color, and beloved pets.

Ingrid Leess has fashioned a lamp for a dining room console from an old porch balustrade using a "Make-a-Lamp Kit" from a local hardware store.

New Scandinavian design chairs are upholstered in a floral crewel fabric that provides a nice textural contrast with the white-painted wood and sisal flooring.

Gerbera daisies, their single stems contained in antique pharmaceutical bottles, provide a whimsical note and a nice play of color and texture against the linens in Julia Turshen's bedroom.

Decorative pillows in vintage-feel florals and a wide ticking stripe would add a romantic element to any room, especially when trimmed with dressmaker detail, fringe, self-welt, and ruffles.

The juxtaposition of textures, the crackled glaze of a classic-shaped celadon lamp on wood pedestal with linen shade, a spiky-shaped conch shell, and the glass and steel construction of a campaign-style occasional table evoke a peaceful romance.

Neutral-toned romantic essentials rely on

A delicately scaled slipper chair, upholstered in a glazed cotton chintz, in the romantic dressing room of designer Toni Gallagher.

Silk-embroidered and geometrically pieced throw pillows are neutral-toned to complement many different colors and textures.

A collection of antique silk brocade, striped, and tapestry pillows in my living room enlivens the neutral tweed of my romantically shaped "bullion" sofa.

The flat-weave of an antique Aubusson carpet provides pattern and texture to the wide-planked, dark-stained floor in Toni Gallagher's dining room.

My "Cathay" secretary, a versatile piece of furniture that was inspired by an antique, transforms with styling from desk to display area and bar—here housing my cherished collection of shells, apothecary jars, and vintage bar ware.

Gilt-framed botanical prints depicting single blossoms or whole plants are key essentials in the romantic's repertoire.

texture, shape, and spare pops of color.

A classic French-style salon chair is newly interpreted in a fresh, creamy neutral upholstery, making it an interesting foil to more modern shapes and styles.

A textural composition—a bas-relief frame, a glazed celadon jar, a coarsely woven fringed linen table scarf, and a sculpted silver candlestick lamp —essentials to creating romantic still lifes and vignettes.

A Picasso woman overlooks the bar in this composition of silver and cut-crystal.

Embroidered, striped, and ribbed textural fabrics in gold and platinum tones enhance a romantic palette.

Lemons in a three-tiered black wire stand and a vivid yellow primrose lend a romantic punch of color against a black-and-white toile slipper chair and gingham checked curtains.

Romantic eclecticism expressed in a

Candlestick lamps for mantels, buffets, or dresser tops are freshly embellished with a collection of shades—from Chinese-inspired prints and embroidery to an almost floral-shaped animal print.

Sisal carpeting works in any setting, providing a neutral backdrop on which to place brilliant color or more subdued tones of furniture and accessories.

The symmetry of pairs is a visual tool often used by the romantic decorator—here two Venetian candlesticks-turned-lamps on an antique dresser framed by a pair of Ottoman-striped silk curtains.

Hardware for a romantic's room—blue, lavender, amber, and green curtain finials, tie-backs, drawer pulls, and a porcelain light switch.

Colefax & Fowler silk-striped curtains, a wall sconce, and French porcelain plate in the dressing room of Toni Gallagher.

A circa 1916 watercolor of a society lady, balloon shades in a Rogers & Goffigon stripe, and a 19th-century French settee create an elegantly romantic vignette.

variety of hardware, textures, furniture, and lampshades.

A stylized white faux-bois lamp is framed by a black shade and pedestal in the bedroom of Julia Turshen.

SENSORY BOX

Sight: Toile wallpaper, pillows and throws, chaises and settees
Scent: Ylang ylang, lavender, potpourri
Sound: Steve Tyrell, Diana Krall, Tony Bennett
Touch: Cashmere, rose petals, glazed cotton, embroidery
Taste: Earl Grey, Lapsang Souchong, chamomile teas

The feminine profile of this chair imbues it with romance—the attached seat and back, rolled arms, and turned feet create a classic shape that would work in either a modern or traditional setting.

adventurous

adventurous mood

To me adventurous is fly-fishing in the Battenkill River in southern Vermont. It is a map, a pair of broken-in hiking boots, and two pulling-at-the-leash Westies—my two four-footed trekking pals, Winnie and Lola—with trails to be discovered and vistas to be enjoyed. It is a trip to New Mexico, exploring the Rio Grande and its environs. It's a dip into the intriguing shops of Chinatown in San Francisco or a peek at my brother-in-law Ron's marvelous design studio in Princeton, New Jersey.

Adventurous is a *Baedeker* (I love that name), a language phrase book, and a pocket full of foreign coins. It exudes heat and spice, shimmering color and exotic flora and fauna. But most of all it is an appreciation of what travel and adventure entail—being introduced to unfamiliar peoples and cultures, experiencing firsthand the way people of other cultures eat, play, interact, work, or worship, absorbing the variety of different habitats and places and coming home with new ideas and inspiration.

As a furniture and textile designer I have visited China and other countries that make up the Pacific Rim. I have visited beautiful rural areas—both here and in the Far East—where the people are as genuine and honest as the goods they manufacture. I've picked up worldly treasures and collectibles, but mostly I have gained experience, lasting memories, and the friendship of some amazing people around the world.

I continue to be seduced by the sights, sounds, smells, fashion, food, music, architecture, and art of other peoples and places. I have also learned to value the skills and craftsmanship in the furniture, fashion, accessories, and artifacts that I've seen around the globe and so adventurous elements continue to find their way into our home.

The dynamics of Adventurous style embrace eclecticism, which allows us to choose from myriad diverse sources and influences to make a design statement that is uniquely and inimitably personal. The adventurous mood in a room is colorfully rich and texturally diverse. It is a style that demands careful editing, organization, and arrangement, and becomes dynamic through rotation and change.

And a tip to remember for those whose traveling days are over, or whose budget is momentarily "stretched," museum shops, art galleries, flea markets, and tag sales can give you a great opportunity to see the world through other people's eyes. And, of course, books—novels, travel books, design books—can bring the world in all its splendor right into your living room.

The Adventurous style embraces eclecticism, allowing us to choose from myriad sources and influences to make design statements that are uniquely and inimitably personal. It is colorfully rich and texturally diverse . . . and, we should remember, requires editing and organization.

Worn leather, vibrant textiles, humble collections of natural objects—rocks, shells, bone fragments, and dried plant material, baskets of baubles, vintage collecting jars, and the patina of an old typewriter and dice—are all fine examples of the textural look and feel of decorating in the adventurous mood. Travel, curiosity, an appreciation for ethnic and handmade artifacts plus the confidence to build a room on the strength of these influences define what adventurous is all about.

adventurous texture

Adventurous texture can capture the experience of travel in a swatch of fabric—an ethnic geometric particular to a culture, a batik wall hanging, an embroidered shawl dripping with a fringe of beads and silk, tiny mirrors sewn along the border. Adventurous style means handcrafted cultural expressions—a hand-carved figurine, a hand-turned urn, the simple form of a hand-coiled pottery bowl or woven basket. Sensual elements of Adventurous are those things you can touch, purchase, and take home with you—the sounds captured on a CD of world music, the tastes inherent in a pungent sauce or a spicy chocolate, and the smells of a fragrant oil, an exotic flower, or a stick of incense.

Travel souvenir texture can be found in the satiny smoothness of an ebony tribal stool or a carved figurine that has been sanded and polished. It can be rough like a boar-bristle brush or a woven coarse basket. Each journey for me provides new memories as well as new souvenirs. From my most recent trip to the Philippines I returned with worn, weathered *santos*, statues of saints reaching out their hands in a welcoming gesture.

In the 19th century it became customary for Europeans and Americans of means to visit the great capitals of Europe, Africa, and Asia. Souvenirs such as those traditionally collected on these grand tours have become the desired collectibles and textures of today—paisley shawls from India and Scotland; prints from Italy; furniture from Paris; porcelain from China, Japan, and France; kente and kuba cloth from Africa; furs from Russia; lamps, rugs, spice boxes, beds, tables, paintings, and art from Morocco, Persia, Afghanistan, and India. Natural specimens—insects, butterflies, birds, and their eggs—were also collected and arranged in specially designed cases.

Today, of course, we are more ecologically aware of the consequences of disturbing animal and plant life. Luckily, today there is a vast array of home accessories in faux animal prints and furs and resin accessories that mimic antler and horn.

A sense of texture can also be found in the way ordinary objects are used in unexpected ways—a pile of books as an end table, a vibrantly painted Moroccan table in a traditionally styled room, a lacquered rice basket that holds necessities in the bathroom.

In adventurous styling these treasures become the passport, or key, to the personality of that space. By arranging and displaying these possessions with a sensitivity not just to texture but also color, balance, and weight, objects from all over the world and from many different times and places can be viewed and appreciated in a harmonious whole.

adventurous color & pattern

In my living room, inspiration from my travels has helped me break out of my inclination for pure serenity. I have filled my room with color, albeit monochromatic, but in a glorious shade of squash that borders on burnished saffron or gold.

Adventurous colors are from the earth, mixed with the vitality of various cultures—the cultivated crops, herbs, dyes, fashion, foods, and spices. These shades are layered, complex, and as individual as the pattern of whorls on a leopard's skin or the stripes on a zebra.

If monochromatic denotes serene, and a splay of related colors and florals express the joyful, full-of-life attitude of romantic, then adventurous is certainly expressed in the contrast of colors, their different weights and complements that add mystery and exoticism, and in the punch of primary color for emphasis and accent. These tones are darker than romantic, more autumn-rich than jaunty spring. You can recognize the style instantly by strong patterns, such as the light and dark contrast of an exotic animal, and the daring use of assertive color: the reds (garnet, oxblood, or coral), dark blue, the greens (forest, khaki, and emerald), the deep golden hues of honey and straw, and richness of the browns.

Travel can be a great starting point for selecting fabric and patterns to use in your home. I once visited a fabric house in an Italian village where the same family was making the exact handcrafted, quality fabric they had produced for hundreds of years. I came home with enough yardage of gorgeous woven velvet to make four sofa pillows.

But even if you can't travel to find your own wonderful fabric souvenirs, don't despair; they're everywhere. Kilims, once the trademark of exotic trips or a "to the trade only" fabric house, are now abundantly available and showing up not only as rugs but also as upholstery for chairs, mixed with leather on sofas, as floor cushions, or backed with velvet as sofa pillows.

I believe, like other designers before me, notably Elsie de Wolfe, that animal-skin prints with their contrasting, graphic colors act almost as neutrals in an adventurous setting and can be an interesting foil to strong, solid colors or to more varied paisleys, kilims, floral patterns, ticking stripes, kuba and kente cloth, and other ethnic prints for a very exotic look.

Tropical plants and botanicals, animals such as monkeys, giraffes, and elephants, maps, and African- and Asian-design motifs and patterns all suggest exotic travel and make for interesting printed fabrics for upholstery, pillows, and bedding.

This home is about cultural melding—an adobe home in New Mexico that mixes the pitched-roof, beamed vernacular of the rural Northeast with the wide-open spaces of a European country house. It is a perfect symbol for the marriage of the owners, one of whom hails from New England and the other from Saint Petersburg, Russia. They call their home "Misha."

Rich color is an important design element in this adventurous room. As designer Stephen Beili explains it, "Color plays off the various hues cast by the sun as it makes its way across the endless southwestern desert sky." Earth tones abound in this space—the clay color of the fireplace wall is a nod to the traditional adobe, while the yellow floating wall demarcates the kitchen area of the house and reflects the sunlight streaming in from the open portal. Primitive furniture and simple handmade accessories recede, allowing the architecture of the room to take precedence. Unexpectedly, the harlequin check of the club chair and the heavier abstract floral on the sofa are mixed with the deep, intense colors of a Persian rug—again a nod to more European opulence. The textural elements of natural materials are rich and varied—stucco walls, a stone mantel, the carved wood of the built-in cabinet, and the formidable look of the saguaro cactus are part of this adventurous mix.

Color is a key adventurous design element, playing off various hues cast by the sun.

The perfect spot to light a fire and watch the
colors of the sunset.

When an opera singer, accustomed to the sumptuous houses of Europe and the exotic travel of her tours, decides to put down roots, she does so with a grand gesture. Regina Rickless built this outdoor living room alongside the kitchen of her mountain home near Santa Fe. Designed by John Midyette, it is crafted out of ponderosa pine logs. Notable for the "leopard peeling" on the beams or *vigas*, the ceiling logs are arranged in a sunburst pattern, a fitting New Mexican emblem.

Tray tables that Regina picked up in Morocco, porcelain purchased in England, sheepskin from Australia, and accessories from Mexico and Spain add an adventurous layer to this sun-splashed space.

Rickless favors earth tones and soft shades. "I like an eclectic look," she says. "I love using the pieces my late husband and I picked up in Europe and mixing them with other indigenous pieces—ones that come with a history, background, or pedigree."

"I have traveled all over the world," says shopkeeper and homeowner Nicole Keane. "I would always fall in love with so many things and I brought home what I could. My husband used to joke that I would rather leave my clothes behind than a painting or an artifact that caught my eye." Keane firmly believes that if you buy what you love and you fall in love for the right reasons—that no matter what you lug back from your travels, it will work in your home. In this intimate seating area, 19th-century botanicals from Spain dress up and lend color to the painted white stone of the fireplace. The French candlesticks on the mantel were electrified, and the wicker chairs have been repainted numerous times and made comfortable with fitted cushions. The desk was custom-made by Dick Whitman, a Wisconsin artist of renown. The plaid, pinch-pleated curtains are trimmed with a contrasting fringe and hung from simple wooden rods.

Keane shows her knack for creating an adventurous still life, a composition of pleasing proportions, textures, and objects. "Varied textures are the key to any room's fascination. It's not only the mix of fabric, it's bringing in stone, bird's-eye maple, birch, wicker, pine, lacquer—these are the things that keep the look dynamic."

"Varied textures are the key to any room's fascination."

An adventurous still life

a composition of pleasing proportions, textures, and objects.

Subdued colors provide a neutral

This was the living room where my husband and I raised our family before we moved to our new home. It evokes memories of playing games in front of the fire, or reading together with the boys on our laps.

The colors are a subdued adventurous palette—creams, beiges, browns on the walls, rug, and furniture, accented with black that provides a neutral backdrop for a collection of cherished souvenirs we've gathered from around the world. Patterns abound, whether on the animal-print upholstery, pillows, throws, or rugs. There is a warm patina to the black tole boxes from England, pencil boxes from Istanbul, and a pair of early-19th-century saffron gold Italian lyre-back chairs with a touch of their former gilt underneath. Two favorite paintings—English landscapes circa 1820—face two wood columns from an old sailing ship and are catty-corner to our antique library table. An antique market basket from France enriches a simple glass and metal coffee table.

OPPOSITE: these same essentials—our furniture, art, and travel souvenirs—make the transition from our old home to the new one beautifully.

backdrop for a collection of souvenirs.

This is my new living room, markedly different in size and shape from my old one, but I'm pleased to say I was able to recycle most of that room's furniture—creating a new look that really works for us. My oversized sofa is the focal point—floating in the center of the room, dividing the long space into two: an intimate seating area and a more open and airy entryway with library table and an ottoman in front. Our leopard-print slipper chairs again face each other across a jute rug. The columns were positioned to add drama and divide the room. I did replace the coffee table (the other was too large for this smaller space) and brought in one of my leather upholstered benches, covering it with a beaded throw from my collection. The Italian lyre-back chairs are unseen at the entryway to the room. Carved wooden *santos* from the Philippines were picked up on my recent travels to that country and are in the same place they were in my old living room. Color is what really lends this space an adventurous air. At night it is a spicy saffron. During the daylight it is pure gold. I was fortunate to find ready-made drapes in that same colorway. Their silk organdy overlay adds an additional layer of texture and voluptuousness while bamboo shades underneath add to the adventurous spirit.

Furniture, fabrics, rugs, and accessories are some of the key ingredients that Los Angeles designer Lynn von Kersting weaves so effortlessly into the mix of her signature rooms.

This cozy, intimate conversation area looks as though it were lifted from a vintage Moroccan tea room. On one side of the room three bold red-and-white checked chairs are pulled up to a vibrant kilim-covered card table; a banquette seat along a half wall provides seating for the fourth. Two low, loosely slipcovered sofas filled with cushions and pillows face each other. A pair of black Indonesian-style chairs face the rose-covered window where a daybed does double duty as banquette seating and coffee table. Color-ful and bold embellishments are set off against a neutral background of barely tinted walls and muted silk curtains. Here, the adventurous look is honed in the details—animal-print pillows and an upholstered bench, a Moroccan inlaid end table, a paisley-covered lamp shade, Persian rugs on par-quet floors—and flowers abound, bright bunches of garden roses, hydrangeas, and pansies.

A cozy, intimate conversation area looks as though it were lifted from a vintage Moroccan tea room.

Lynn von Kersting has been a design inspiration to me for many years. I never fail to return from visits to her California shop, Indigo Seas, without bringing home ideas and objects that she has collected from around the world. She is fearless in her ability to layer textiles and gets the mix just right. In a detail from a living room she designed in Bel Air, antique pillows are piled on a toile sofa—the same patterned fabric also upholstered onto the walls. An ebony standing lamp with a brilliant red shade and tassel trim punctuates the scene, while an antique painted Chinese trunk serves as a coffee table.

RIGHT: A pair of Kashmiri candlesticks with 19th-century silk shades top stacks of rare and out-of-print books in her own library. Fragrant rosemary lends an adventurous waft of scent.

How to get this look

0—⊸ Display books; they are inherently interesting and make your rooms come to life.

0—⊸ Use sprigs of herbs and small bowls of spice for a scented, sensual touch.

0—⊸ Prop up your paintings for a bit of adventure—they don't have to be hung on a wall.

LEFT: Delicately framed 19th-century hand-lettered astrological charts are hung in a vertical line in our entryway. I love these prints. They greet my visitors with an air of mystery while adding architectural interest.

BELOW: This small book hutch is another of my furniture designs. Nestled into a corner in our tiny den, I use it to display travel souvenirs, hand-bound volumes, and other treasured artifacts.

LEFT: "We bought this antique Irish sideboard years ago from Chris Mead in Bridgehampton," explains Doug Turshen. "We used it in our dining room in the Hamptons and again when we moved to this 1840s Greek Revival house. But after a while we realized that what this rather large powder room needed was a real piece of furniture to give it weight and character. The sideboard just happened to be the perfect thing. We installed a sink and vintage faucets." It has a lovely patina, interesting silhouette, display ledges for symmetrical arrangements of flowers, and drawers for soaps and hand towels, and because of its proximity to the dining room, it serves as storage for extra linens.

RIGHT: I have devoted two walls of our dining room into a gallery for my menus—a collection that not only showcases the graphics and design of the documents but also highlights the culinary expertise of the chefs and serves as an artful reminder of splendid evenings. Menus include one from a Paris bistro, another one from Venice commemorating a second honeymoon trip with Kevin, and a little diner menu from a trip to San Francisco with our boys. In each case the chef was delighted to give us a menu, signing and dating them as well. They're hung asymmetrically, expanding horizontally as I fill the space. Nothing matches except the gold of the frames. For our family these walls are an expression of love and good-food memories.

LEFT: A bookcase is built into this corner space in Lynn von Kersting's library. Here an old Moroccan pillow, with embroidery bearing the sultan's signature and lantern, shares the space with a worn French leather chair.

Like most adventurous rooms, this one was not designed so much as it evolved. It contains inherited items—an old oak table that was stored in an Iowa barn for fifty years and a console table that once graced a New York City apartment—along with some unusual treasures: a twig chair and a standing lamp, a folk art carving of the Liberty Bell, and ethnic artifacts such as the vintage kilim rug used as a table cover and multiple patterned benches used as coffee and end tables.

The owners, Andy and Carolyn Schultz, have a love of the handmade and for the beauty in found objects such as turkey feathers, birch bark, and sea biscuits collected on trips around the United States from the woods of Washington to the rocky shores of Maine. They like the artifacts in their home to tell a story. The wicker chair was a gift from a Nobel Prize winner, while another friend designed the paisley sofa. The blue ginger jar lamp is from a New York City thrift shop. A cigar box holds Carolyn's father's eighth-grade science project—a sampling of rocks from around his state.

The buttery gold walls and sage linen curtains help elevate the light and mood in this artifact-filled space.

Strong color, contrast, and bold accessories play off the textural backdrop of raffia wallcovering and a low-pile wool rug, making this small New York City apartment study sizzle. Designed by Stephen Miller Siegel for his friend and client Stephen Jacoby, the study is in harmony with the rest of the apartment's background texture, but the adventurous appointments break this room out of the subdued color scheme. The most striking visual element is the zebra-patterned ottoman used as both a coffee table and a footrest. It gives the room weight and, as one oversized object often does, makes the space appear larger. Jonathan Adler–designed geometric pillows and Russian constructivist magazine covers accentuate this adventurous mood.

My den, with its backdrop of glazed red walls, is filled with my family's extensive collection of Broadway *Playbill*s, CDs, and rare and first-edition books. It is also home to comfortable furniture pieces we've owned forever but that have been reupholstered many times. A wedding basket from China serves as an end table. And in keeping with my adventurous spirit, a vintage globe bar is the perfect functional accessory.

In my dining room, shells we've collected from beaches around the world are displayed with antique specimen bottles in one of my favorite pieces from my furniture collection, a chinoiserie secretary. Seashells in a pedestal dish are a departure from the more expected floral arrangement in the table's center. Elegant yet sturdy paisley chairs with nail-head trim surround a table I designed. A sisal rug, textured walls, and soft, golden-hued curtains provide a textural backdrop to tie together the many eclectic, albeit adventurous, elements.

How to get this look

0—☛ Hang a mirror beside a window to enlarge a small space.

0—☛ Glaze a room with a deep, rich red to evoke a feeling of intimacy.

0—☛ Mix, don't match, your dinnerware for an adventurous table setting.

The room has character, combining local
quarried stone with whitewashed, rough-hewn timber.

Once the center of a working carriage house, this is the room that first attracted us when we saw our new home. Where the window is now was once the entryway for horses and buggies of the last century.

Its age and character have all the elements of adventure—combining local quarried stone in a charcoal hue with whitewashed, rough-hewn timber. Large stone columns divide the space into two areas: one square, the other rectangular. I followed that lead, turning one side into a cozy dining area defined with my round table and the same paisley chairs (see page 95) now slipcovered in a tailored, monogrammed white cotton duck. The table is flanked on either side by my "bibliothèque" bookcases that I loved creating. On the other side of the room, my farmhouse table houses stacks of design books and favorite objects. When I'm entertaining large parties, this table is swept clean—allowing the room to seat up to eighteen people comfortably.

The dining area is more English in style, but with an adventurous twist—an antler chandelier from New Mexico shares airspace with a high shelf holding blue-and-white dishes from Japan. The black lacquer secretary is 19th-century English and is a great display space for all the "smalls" in Keane's collection—porcelain boxes from France, china hand-painted by her mother and aunt, inkwells and miniature treasures from around the world. The table skirt is a favorite Schumacher silk with a subtle tattersall border for a bit of dressmaker detail.

"I don't care if I only live in one room, it is going to be the most magnificent room full of things that I have found and fallen in love with," says Nicole Keane of her cottage behind her home-furnishing shop, N. Keen & Co. in Manchester, Vermont. The cottage was formerly a carriage house for a postman's horse and delivery wagon. "I used to live in a very grand house and most of my things are now in storage. But what was so fun about decorating this space was editing my collection, finding the perfect pieces to fit, and still tell the story of my travels. I've been everywhere . . . on every continent. Now I'm trying to settle down with only things that have meaning to me." The kitchen is evocative of French country with its oil-jar lamp, Provencal-inspired shade, copper molds, and white stoneware. A hallway into the kitchen area contains Asian furniture, a unique bamboo étagère plant stand used for candles, and a mix of framed prints.

"If you **love something**, you can make it work in a room."

Despite being barely thirty-something, Helen Gunn has held jobs in Glasgow, London, Amsterdam, and New York. A native of the U.K., she now lives in Greenwich, Connecticut, in a Victorian-era garret apartment. Her bedroom reflects her penchant for travel and her ability to mix textures, fabrics, patterns, and shapes to create compositions that are colorful, exciting, and personally meaningful. Her bed is one of the first objects she ever bought for the various spots she has called home, and it traveled with her from the States to the U.K. and back again. Along the way she acquired the accoutrements of a seasoned traveler—the shawl is from Scotland, the duvet from Scandinavia, and the embroidered pillow from France. Above her dresser hangs a Moroccan lantern, and a printer's drawer from Maine holds her miniature treasures and charms, silver and gold replicas of the Leaning Tower of Pisa, the Eiffel Tower, Big Ben, and the Statue of Liberty, to name but a few.

A garret apartment reflects the owner's penchant for travel and **mixing textures,** fabrics, and patterns.

adventurous essentials

Because Adventurous style emphasizes eclecticism, choosing from different sources and cultures, there is endless variety in the essentials that make this look. These spaces exude life and vitality. You can add an adventurous touch to your upholstered furniture using fabrics and patterns. Or you can use simple, neutral fabrics and patterns as a backdrop, popping in the adventurous touch with kilim, or tribal stools and benches, Chinese painted trunks or lacquered baskets, which effectively serve as side and coffee tables or storage and accent pieces. Your furniture finishes can be rustic, painted, dark stained, or stripped. Furniture can mix materials and fabric—a leather sofa with tapestry cushions, a wooden daybed with a woven rattan bottom.

Window treatments explore the mix—bamboo shades with billowy silk curtains, paisley valances, silk saris, simple ethnic prints, or loosely woven textiles made from natural plant fibers.

Lamps and lighting fixtures are varied and eclectic—wood-turned standing floor lamps with ornate shades dripping with beads or brass and metal pharmacy lamps. Oversized olive oil jar lamps, urns, ceramics, galvanized clamp lamps, Moroccan architectural lamps, electrified oil lamps, or traditional outdoor lighting fixtures brought indoors also fit the adventurous bill.

Lampshades are of various materials, patterns, and textures—burlap, brown, black or white, animal prints, velvet, silk, beaded, or embellished.

An assortment of rugs and flooring materials signal adventurous styling, such as kilims from desert tents, Navajo serapes, bold stripes, rich Persians, fur, animal skin, or simple sisal. These rugs can be layered over slate, concrete, vinyl, stone, or wood, all good choices, or these floorings can stand alone, unadorned.

Anything can be a travel souvenir worthy of bringing home—fabric tapestries, runners, throws and pillows, books, baskets, handmade cultural artifacts, ethnic crafts and arts, shells, pressed botanicals, rock, stone, or sand. Candles bought in your travels can look culturally inspired and varied, scented with ethnic spice or perfume.

Your objects can be grouped by subject—natural history objects, a bowl of shells, books, figurines—or displayed as vignettes, the shapes and textures playing off one another. They can be displayed asymmetrically on either side of a mantel or as rigorously aligned as a natural history museum display, categorized by size, shape, color, and level of detail.

Any room is not complete without the sensory elements, and adventurous styling is no exception—it needs that touch of spice. Wherever I travel, I invariably fall in love with the sounds and music I hear around me. I seek out recordings as audio reminders of that trip. I also tend to visit specialty food shops so I can bring home the tastes of my travels and share them with my family. After a trip to New Mexico, I came home with bags of dried chilis, salsas, and piquant spiced nuts. Scents can be captured in incense and perfume, infused into a fabric, sewn into a sachet, or captured in a fragrant soap.

An 18th-century Spanish reliquary opens up to reveal a collection of cherished antique books, turned wooden goblets, and an inkwell—sailor's art from Capri in the Schultz living room.

Adventurous lamp-shades explore texture and materials—pleated paper, wicker and woven grasses, embroidered silk and fabric.

Colorful and variously textured fixtures

Etched colored glass mixed with clear panes in this multi-faceted lamp create a riot of pattern and color when lit from within with candlelight and suspended from the ceiling.

Bamboo blinds, various textured and patterned pillows, an earthenware lamp, and a reclining sculpture create an adventurous vignette.

A French linen pillow, an Afghan kilim rug table cover, a vintage yellow pitcher from New Mexico, a found moose antler from Maine, a Moroccan lantern, and an English landscape painting are the essentials of this still life.

A red-glass bell jar ceiling fixture is a reproduction of an 18th-century model from the Oriental Lamp Shade Company.

An oversized olive oil jar lamp provides ambient lighting in this small kitchen. An animal print ceramic dog dish fits the Adventurous style.

allow adventurous vignettes to glow with ambient light.

Sculptural garden elements—an angel and a large urn—share space with more tradi-tional elements in this study.

The American lantern, a hurricane appropriate for indoor or outdoor use, is from the Met-ropolitan Museum of Art gift shop.

Edward Curtis photographs and a found animal skull provide contrasting texture on this lime-stone and adobe mantel.

A vintage seltzer bottle made into a lamp complete with a white linen shade in the home of Nicole Keane.

Adventurous trim in ethnic prints, bright colors, coarse weaves, and silky fringes are details that embellish pillows and upholstery.

A mesquite wood table holds a scrolled metal candelabra and a brightly glazed ceramic lamp from Mexico at the Rickless home in Santa Fe.

Adventurous is ethnic inspirations,

A metal bamboo bed and a West Indies-inspired settee in the bedroom of our home. Bamboo poles are used as curtain rods.

A cotton kilim rug with hand-knotted fringe inspired by a Moroccan design displays the adventurous color palette.

Benjamin Moore's flat-finish Regal Wall Satin paint in #070 helps create the bones of a spicy-hued adventurous room.

Simple linen tab-top curtains hang from hardware fashioned from fallen tree limbs in this Montana home.

Linen curtains are almost sheer when the sun comes in behind them. *Doors of Santa Fe* color photographs, two in a series by photographer Jay Gold.

Coarsely woven grasscloth, linen, and chunky knits are some of the textures in the adventurous collection of throws and pillows.

natural fibers and materials, and spicy rich color.

A faux bamboo and wicker safari chair folds to be easily transported whether in the wilderness or in a living room.

A recessed niche in the interior living room wall of this Southwestern home provides the perfect spotlighted display area for sculpture or other art.

Natural slate is a flooring essential for the adventurous spirit.

A collection of hand-woven, ethnic-inspired baskets and totes provide textural dimension hanging from this ceiling's rafters.

Espresso and natural linen colors, here in coarsely woven textural fabrics, are some of the neutral essentials for adventurous styling.

A curvy, natural wicker table has a handgrip on the top, making it easy to move about the room for seating or extra table space.

Worn leather, wood rich with a golden patina, and velvety smooth felt cowboy hats are all part of this Western-flavored still life.

Unusual shapes, the look of the handmade, rich color,

A 19th-century church pew, softened with an ethnic print pillow, offers seating at the library/dining table in the Schultz living room.

A large wool runner in yellow and red awning stripe with a contrasting green border coordinates with the hues in the adventurous palette.

In this garden/mud room, a rustic chair provides a spot to slip on boots, while a watering can, fashioned from concrete and inset with a mosaic of broken crockery, provides whimsy.

A tapered teak ladder is a reproduction of a 19th-century English apple-picking implement. It can be used as a mobile shelving unit for books or to display objects.

Leather, tapestry, and cotton duck, all in rich dark hues, provide interesting fabric choices for adventurous upholstery.

A folding bamboo chair is functional, lightweight, and portable for seating indoors and out.

and the beauty in found objects.

My new living room with the varied mix of pattern and fabrics. Bamboo shades from Smith and Noble provide contrast to the luxurious silk drapes. Ticking stripes share floor space with animal prints.

A still life display in the Schultz living room features a folk art sculpture of the Liberty Bell, a sea biscuit displayed on an amber pedestal, and a cigar box containing a vintage science project.

serene

serene mood

Let's try an easy exercise to discover your serene zone. Close your eyes and conjure the most peaceful setting you can imagine—an ocean beach or a glowing sunset, a quiet chapel or a room somewhere that spoke to you of quiet calm, a showcase house or a nursery with a sleeping child. Let your imagination carry you away.

Now take a moment to think about that visual you just created. What vacation spot, spa, restaurant, memory, or occasion did you conjure? Since that is how you picture serenity, use the mood of that place—the colors, sounds, smells, textures, tastes, or furnishings—as the inspiration in creating your own serene home.

We know in design it is not just about how something looks but also how it feels. If you visualized a favorite restaurant, for example, it was not only the décor and table settings that created the mood, it was the music, the lighting, the shape of the dishes, the feel of the glass, and the tastes you put in your mouth that made for a memorable experience.

Or if you thought of late-afternoon waves crashing on the shore, it might not be just the colors of the sea and sky, but also the rough texture of the sand, the smell of the salt air, or the feel of sea spray on your face that enhanced the mood.

Because my life is, at times, like so many of yours, filled with multitasking moments, I've tried to create serenity in the more intimate areas of my house—the bedroom and bathroom. I've done this by trying to avoid clutter—it makes me feel stressed to see a lot of stuff—and concealing necessities with unique storage solutions. Quietude for me means that too many things aren't "jumping out at me," including color. I use various shades of white—the creams and taupes—for my bedding, curtains, walls, and rugs. Loved ones appear in black-and-white photographs, hanging in matching frames on cream-colored walls.

I use objects that I love—old glass jars, lacquered boxes, and small silver trays and condiment bowls—for texture and containment of the stuff of life. Music—early jazz, classical guitar, and soulful ballads—is important in helping me relax and refocus on my life away from work, at home. So, too, are lovely scents—the herbal fragrances of rosemary and garlic when we're cooking dinner in our kitchen, or the scented candle I light whenever we get to sit in our living room and relax. In the quiet of my bedroom I luxuriate in fine fabrics—the crisp cotton of our sheets, the soft throw at the foot of the bed, even the rougher terry cloth of my bathrobe. But nothing is like the feel of Winnie's and Lola's fur as I give them a final pat good night.

Water, sunlight, and shadow; warm neutrals; and simple honest shapes all bespeak quiet serenity. Objects appear singularly or in pleasing arrangements where symmetry and balance are key.

In a serene mood where color and pattern are subdued, textures, shapes, and the contrast of light and dark take on more importance. Inspiration for serenity comes from nature—here water plays an important role—the calm of the sea, the warmth from the bath. The palette is that found in nature, the color of water, aged wood, sandstone, eggshell, sea grass, clay, and the browns and greens of the earth. The look and feel is quiet, there's nothing to surprise or "jump out." Serene interiors inspire you to sit back, take a deep breath, and let go of daily stresses.

serene texture

To me, comfort is the key ingredient in any room, and in a serene space comfort emerges from a mix of subtle textures that are soft and luxurious, pleasurable to the hand and to the eye.

Solid wools, silks, cashmere, mohair, leather, velvet, and organdy sheers are all serene and luxurious fabric choices. There is a resurgence, thank goodness, of great synthetics due, in large part, to the influences and influx of materials from abroad, so you can also achieve the serene look by buying some good imitations of cashmere and leather or some cotton and silk blends. Or, you can combine one luxurious piece—a beautiful throw, pillow, or rug—with the more prosaic but practical cotton duck slipcover or sisal rug.

If you were able to visualize your serene place clearly, you could probably make a list of the essential items in that room. This is because serenity speaks succinctly, using the same principles as graphic design—employing contrast and simple, clean shapes against a neutral space to get across a word or an idea.

As in graphic design, serene space is punctuated with accent strokes. In interiors, this stroke could be a low, clean-cut sofa; a white, sculptural lamp on an ebony table; or a throw contrasting colorwise with a duvet cover on a bed. "Form follows function" is a popular saying in design, and objects employed in the Serene style should be both simple and useful—form and utility in equal measure. Visual and tactile stimulation come in the juxtaposition of textures—hard against soft, gloss against matte, glass against wood, weave against leather, and from the fabrics borrowed from menswear fashions—the herringbones, tweeds, heathered weaves, and nubby berbers. Like serene colors, wonderful materials used in this style are those found in nature— wood, stone, clay, plaster, and glass or plants such as hemp, bamboo, cotton, and reed.

In my own home, I love the contrast of textures provided by the use of a simple sisal carpet, and in the cold months of winter I dress it up with the addition of a wool or silk area rug on top. I delight in the look and feel of my favorite seashells arranged on a matte-painted mantel and plush chenille pillows against the smooth metal of my bed—serene texture at its best!

serene color & pattern

I love the serenity of the understated, natural, and pastel colors found in nature, particularly those in a field of swaying wheat or along the ocean shore. My eye finds rest in the colors of sand, earth, sky, and stone—tan, brown, gray blues, and creamy whites. These tones are calm, organic, peaceful.

A monochromatic color scheme appeals most to me for my private or personal spaces. I like using just one color in multiple tones and shades—usually three, from the deepest tones of brown to the lightest shades of that color: tan, a pale linen, or barely tinted white. Shades of celadon or gray would work as well.

These monochromatic schemes help the eye to settle down and allow the shapes of furniture, artwork, and architecture to stand out.

Serene patterns enable you to bring in other colors without upsetting the monochromatic scheme. Tone-on-tone checks and stripes, for instance, are a great way to express a monochromatic palette, such as in a tan, brown, and white check or a tone-on-tone stripe that stretches from gray to its lighter shades in a room.

Remember, also, that cool colors like ice blue will help set the stage for a serene space much more strongly than hot colors like persimmon, paprika, and bright yellow.

Having worked with many photographers over the years, I have really come to appreciate natural light and its effects on color in a room. Light highlights and changes colors and creates shadows. It alternately softens color or makes it appear brighter, and it helps bring out the subtle gradations of pattern and texture. Texture affects color also in that a palette is expressed differently depending on how the light reflects off that particular texture. Think of how white reflects light differently on a coarse, nubby linen than on a smooth silk, for example.

In a serene space, pattern shouldn't be complicated or too fussy. Graphic or geometric patterns work in serenity because they can reinforce color and mood better than, say, a pattern that is busy with flowers or animals, allowing the entire room to work as a calming oasis.

Designer Bill Cook of Atlanta used a continental mix of mid-century classics in furniture, art, lighting, and accessories to lend this room a modern, graphic design appeal that, while stimulating to the eye, is serene and calming in its overall effect.

With a notable absence of pattern, lighter tones and textures balance the contrasting hues of black and white. Webbed chairs, a mohair-covered sofa with faux fur pillows, a blond sculptural coffee table, a pickled-ash side table used as a bar, and the natural wood tones of the waxed floor and exposed ceiling beams—all neutral colors—help unify the space. The marshmallow sofa by 1950s designer George Nelson adds the visual punch the designer was looking for.

Bill renovated this traditional 1950s ranch house by removing restrictive walls and raising the ceiling. The sense of light and air, the contrast of tones, and the interplay of geometric shapes all contribute as strongly to the visual dynamics as the mid-century treasures he collects.

How to get this look

0—▼ Display black-and-white photography for its crisp, graphic appeal.

0—▼ Incorporate a mix of modern furniture styles, but keep them all clean lined and low in profile.

0—▼ Add pillows with a sense of whimsy or strong texture to soften the edges in a contemporary room.

0—▼ Put all lighting on dimmers to set a serene stage at night.

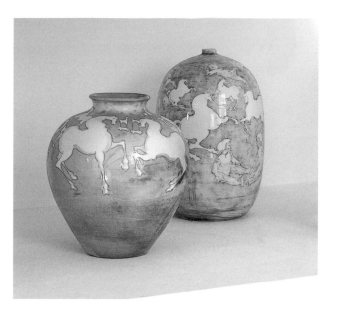

Expansive rooms of white, tinted with the reflected hue of the lakeside blues and greens and punctuated with strokes of brilliant art, are the defining elements in the disciplined and serene home of Bob Sweet. Close friends and adjoining neighbors, the architects Warren Arthur and Mai Tsao, who designed and built the house, share Sweet's design philosophy, and are sympathetic to his insistence on white. "White is what I live with, it is the perfect backdrop for my art collection. White also lets the line and form of objects speak clearly." Sweet's home is a showcase of mid-century modern design—furniture by Eero Saarinen and Mies van der Rohe for Knoll; art by Harry Bertoia, George Rickey, Bobby Cadwallader, former president of Knoll furniture, and Edwina Sandys; and vintage Orrefors crystal and Italian pottery. The absence of overt pattern is balanced by the strong artwork. Sweet introduces some texture with the nubby wool wall-to-wall carpeting and leather upholstered pieces. The chrome-and-glass furniture used throughout the space seems to float seamlessly in these rooms.

FOLLOWING PAGE: A Saarinen table in the entrance hall is backed by a tapestry created by a world-renowned local artist, Helena Hernmarck. Here Sweet demonstrates how white can be warmed with just the introduction of one or two colors or objects. Mies Van der Rohe's Barcelona chaise sits in a window nook with corded silk window treatments affording privacy from the lake beyond. A one-of-a-kind lamp designed by Philip Johnson and Richard Kelley stands at the end of the seating.

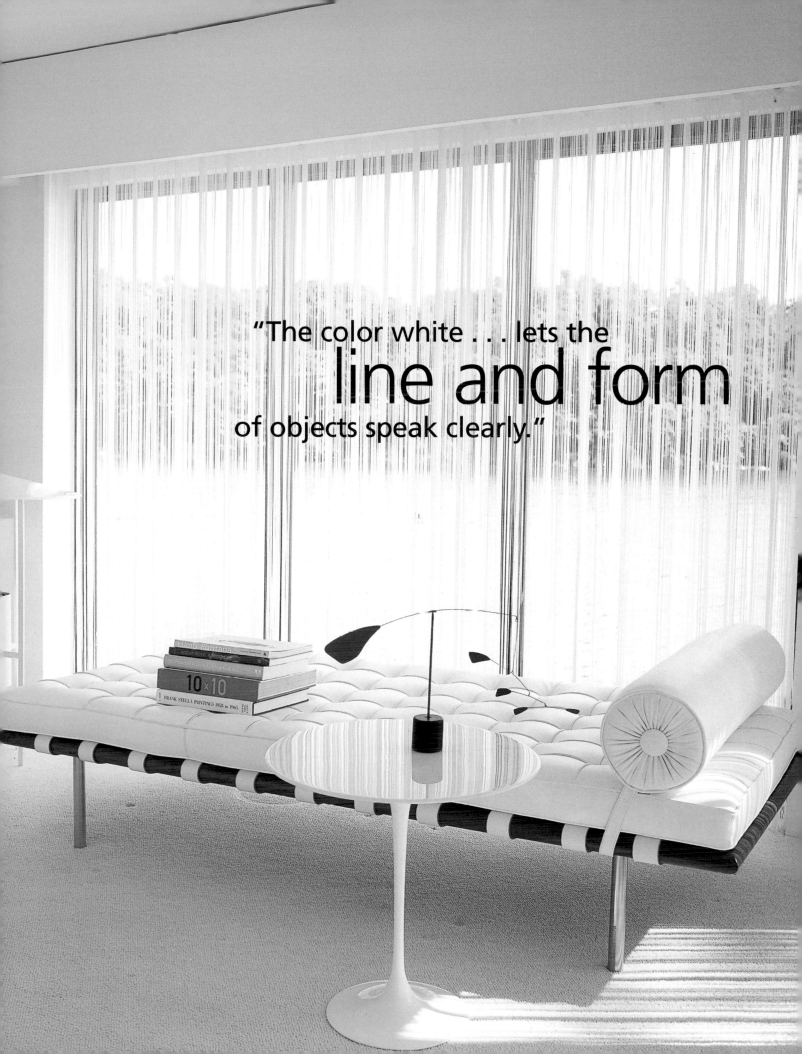

"The color white . . . lets the
line and form
of objects speak clearly."

The design
was influenced
by the light that
saturates this
mountaintop . . .
this room
captures that.

"When a house is built in a setting like this—with incredible mountain
views, outcroppings of rock, and tall
pines—it is so breathtakingly serene,
your interiors have to follow suit,"
explains Tinatin Kilaberidze, who
designed this house as a getaway for a
New York family. "I have to add that the
design was also influenced by the
incredible sunlight that saturates this
mountaintop in northern New England.
This room captures that." It's also a nod
to the simplicity and craftsmanship of
the country. The fireplace is built of local
stone—each carefully placed by a gifted
mason. Its white, blue, gray, and cream
overtones influenced the palette of the
entire room. Decorative objects crafted
from natural elements, like the coverlet
on the sofa back, the earthenware jugs,
and the weathervane, are handmade,
reinforcing the serene ambiance.

This room radiates quietly, in muted,
understated colors
that emphasize texture.

"As a designer, what is important to me is the quality of sunlight in a room," says Ingrid Leess. "I am interested in making rooms as bright as possible." This formerly dark room radiates light yet does so quietly, in muted, understated fabrics that emphasize texture rather than color, creating a space that is visually serene.

She painted the dark paneling a pure white and replaced heavy drapes with simple, diaphanous linen sheers. A two-tone scheme based on the honey color of a collection of baskets and the whiteness of the ceramics on the mantel warms the room, giving a sense of depth.

"White slipcovers on the sofa are appealing and easy to maintain," explains Leess. "I originally started out with all white slipcovers. But then I decided that the room needed more interest—color and texture, but not too much . . . I wanted restrained sophistication." Leess achieved the look she was after with her oversized tan-and-white buffalo checks and a subdued paisley on the ottoman.

Painted paneling offers a serene backdrop for her treasured objects—a collection of paper-and-ink botanical drawings, black-and-white photos, books, and a wooden bowl picking up the tones of the baskets above. Glass jars lend a clear note to her collections.

A mix of materials and textures, light and dark tones, keeps the neutral color scheme in this New York City apartment dynamic. Furniture, shelving, and accessories maintain a low profile on a thickly coiled and woven banana-fiber carpet. A shelf floats along the wall, offering space for books and meaningful objects from the owner's collection.

A fascination for aviation is a theme that permeates this space; Ezra Stoller's photography of Saarinen's TWA terminal at Kennedy Airport and prized vintage model airplanes reflect homeowner Stephen Jacoby's passion for the tools of flight.

The two-tiered lacquered goatskin coffee table by Karl Springer and the two Lucite occasional tables reflect light—an important element in any serene room. A luxurious gray velvet covers all the upholstered modular pieces in the room, effectively anchoring the perimeters of this space, while the predominant pattern of oversized checks in the silk drapes frames the windows. The ebony bookshelf hung on the walls punctuates the space with a jolt of black.

In designing a room for his client, designer Stephen Miller Siegel struck the balance between a need for serenity in an urban environment and an infusion of the owner's personality and passions.

A **balance** is struck between the need for serenity and the visual stimulation.

"This Connecticut house is not 'on' the water," explains architect Mark Finlay, who recently renovated this early 19th-century structure to bring it up to date *and* make it hurricane proof. "It is literally 'in' it. Its foundation is on a promontory outcropping of rock that juts into the Long Island Sound." The interiors indeed reflect this peaceful locale. Noted designer Victoria Hagan created the space after Finlay finished designing and installing new windows, doors, a roof, and ceilings—all sympathetic to its Tudor roots. Hagan chose furniture that would feel right at home in the original but she provided a serene take on traditional style by upholstering the pieces in soft creams and blue gray, her palette borrowed from the water and rock outcroppings—gray, blue, white, tan, and brown. The carpet, a woven check in the same color palette as the rest of the room, recedes into the space. The drama of the "tray" ceiling and the mullioned windows in an ebony finish keep the perimeters of the room anchored.

How to get this look

- Reupholster furniture in fabrics such as soft flannels, wool mohairs, and gently worn linens.
- Divide a large room with multiple seating areas, upholstered in the same pastel tones.
- Keep your window treatments to a minimum, especially when graced with great views.

. . . the interiors reflect their **peaceful,** watery surroundings . . .

When a celebrity writer and radio personality from the Midwest needed a New York City pied-à-terre, he chose a hometown designer, Tom Gunkelman, who understood his need for a quiet oasis in the midst of midtown bustle. "My client wanted something light and contemporary, soft and with no hard edges—a comfortable place for his family, to raise their small child and entertain a few guests. He also wanted a peaceful place to write when he was in the city."

Gunkelman also had a space issue to address: the long narrow living room needed to serve as library/study, to double as a guest bedroom, and still function as a dining room. His solution? The table under the windows, of Gunkelman's design, reflects an art deco sensibility and is used for both study and dining. A pullout sleeper sofa, covered in a soft Donghia chenille, is used for guests. Rather than incorporate the traditional coffee table, a pair of ottomans were chosen and, like the rest of the furnishings, do double duty, here as both footstool and coffee table. And, because the windows face an interior courtyard— a common dilemma in Manhattan—the designer chose Venetian blinds, allowing light control and privacy.

The long narrow living room
needed to serve as library/study,
to **double** as a guest bedroom,
and still to **function** as a dining room.

With the help of architects Warren Arthur and Mai Tsao, Bob Sweet, the owner of this serene home, does the near impossible: make a working kitchen appear almost completely invisible. They conjured this trick with white—white marble, cabinetry, flooring, and appliances. Different textures help delineate the white, providing color variation depending on the light that is reflected from the morning sun. Fresh market ingredients add pattern and color to this calming oasis.

The dining room continues the theme of serene architectural modernism, except here the white is broken up with an almost equal measure of red. Saarinen-designed chairs surround the white, marble-top table. Two walls open up to the terrace with its view of the lake and the tree-lined shore. White wall-to-wall carpet provides an unbroken flow from one room to the next and continues up to the second floor. Sweet maintains that "with fewer objects to distract the eye, the qualities of design and craftsmanship assume greater importance—the integrity of the art must stand the test of close scrutiny as defined by its placement in my all-white home."

With few objects to distract the eye, the qualities of **design** and **craftsmanship** assume greater importance.

Connecticut architect Mark
Finlay built this shingle-style house incorporating old materials—ceiling beams,
wide-plank floors, brick in the fireplace,
and an antique chandelier—with traditional detailing, board-and-batten wainscoting, simple sconces, and mullioned
windows. The furniture, too, is traditional but imbued with a sense of serenity in its restraint, as seen in a Queen
Anne drop leaf table, the refectory table
sideboard, and the tiered serving cart.
Chairs are upholstered in natural linen,
allowing the shape and form of the chair
to take precedence, balancing rustic textures with new materials. Surfaces are
deliberately left clean and uncluttered.
The total effect is fresh and new because
of Finlay's color choices and the way his
skilled treatment of these antique elements breathes new life into the old.

The **architect's signature** is to give the new the look, patina, and softness of the old.

Honest design and integrity are the hallmarks of this Vermont dining room. Overhead, an oversized 18th-century English lantern provides soft candlelight for family gatherings and dinner parties. Robust Windsor-style chairs were recently crafted in New Hampshire—their linear quality adds a quiet sense of architectural serenity to the room. They flank an antique farmhouse table, generously sized to accommodate family and friends. The corner cupboard, custom-designed by Tinatin Kilaberidze for her clients, is also new. The dishes inside keep with the sophisticated mix of old and new—19th-century brown-and-white transferware alongside 21st-century hand-blown goblets from artisan Simon Pearce. Windows are deliberately unadorned. A simple bouquet of hydrangea from the garden displayed under a naive oil painting are the only other flourishes in this otherwise pure interior.

How to get this look

0—⯈ Make a bold statement with an oversized or elongated table that fills the space. Keep other furniture minimal.

0—⯈ Use an unexpected light fixture—an outdoor lantern instead of the more traditional multi-armed chandelier.

0—⯈ Display a piece of white stoneware, such as a soup tureen, platter, or oversized pitcher, on the table instead of a more structured floral or dried-floral centerpiece.

Designer Louise Drevenstam's
objective for her fashion executive client was clear cut: to create a stylish and "serious" office that would also afford its occupant a sense of quietude in his exciting, demanding, and occasionally frenetic business life. Drevenstam took for her inspiration the pleasing contrast of black and white, light and shadow that is the hallmark of mid-century modern art and fashion photography. The ebony-toned linear furniture is the perfect foil for his well-chosen desk accessories, while a tan sisal carpet provides a break in the contrast of opposite color in this singular space. Monochromatic and calm, uncluttered and undeterred by trend, this is a decisive space—just what the CEO calls for.

The designer found inspiration in the pleasing contrasts of the black-and-white fashion photography.

Judith Driscoll's signature
look combines soft color and pattern
with white background interiors that are
fresh, young, and quiet. As with many
serene spaces, the influence is Scandinavian minimalism—a look determined
by the use of blue, white, tan, and light.
During daylight hours, light is used
almost as a color, accentuating the
painted white of the ceiling, windows,
and walls, softening the other colors in
the room. At night, the contrast between
the ginghams and stripes and the white
background is more acute and less satu-
rated—providing stronger colors. The
interior designer chose the room's elements carefully; a Swedish blanket chest
stands at the end of the bed, its painted
surface of sponged dots a pleasing
contrast to the more graphic stripes and
checks of the curtains and bedding. The
simplicity of a striped cotton rug provides another textural contrast to the
area rug and hardwood floor. The architectural ornaments—a finial, a stack of
rustic benches, and tramp art sculpture—
add quiet sophistication to this clean-
lined space.

How to get this look

0—➤ Limit your color palette but
emphasize pattern and texture for a
more minimal look. Here large and small
ginghams, various width stripes, and a
herringbone work together in the same
blue-and-white color palette.

0—➤ Balance harder textures such as the
iron bed and curtain rods with softer
wood ones like a pine blanket chest or
an upholstered chair.

0—➤ Break up strong horizontal lines—
the bed, curtain rods, a line of pillows—
with vertical elements, such as the
architectural finial and stacking benches.

Light is used almost as a color in this Scandinavian **minimalism—** inspired bedroom.

Wrapped in raffia wallcovering with floor-to-ceiling silk drapes, wall-to-wall wool carpet, and a coverlet of cashmere, this New York City bedroom brings "cocooning" to a new level. Designed by Stephen Miller Siegel for his friend and client Stephen Jacoby, the bedroom is quiet, texturally interesting, monochromatic, and masculine.

A wood shelf floating against a caramel-colored wall provides the perfect display for Jacoby's important collection of modern photography. A Heywood Wakefield chair covered in a simple neutral velvet provides a comfortable reading spot in a corner of the room.

The furnishings are all deliberately low and horizontal in profile. The headboard's geometric topstitching is covered in a buttery leather, while a seascape painting above it, executed in gray and mist blue, adds a serene addition to the room's neutral palette.

His bedside étagère tables have glass shelves, making them appear lighter, and the classic swing-arm lamps seem to float. Each element combines to create the perfect buffer to the city outside.

The furnishings are all deliberately low and horizontal in profile.

serene essentials

For our homes to be serene and comfortable, emotionally rich and sensually fulfilling, they need to be furnished with some practical material goods and the "stuff" we simply can't live without: our collections, books, art, technology, and toys. Still, serene rooms demand the most careful editing of these essentials. After all, serenity asks that we avoid clutter and keep objects visually interesting but useful.

Serene furniture is often low and linear in profile, horizontally structured to stay close to the floor. It employs simple geometric forms—boxy and rectangular, circular or arched shapes.

Upholstered furniture exposes legs and often arms and back as well. The materials used to make furniture include dark and blond woods, bamboo, steel, chrome, metal, plastic, and woven grasses. The transparency of glass and acrylic is an important addition to these rooms.

Storage solutions are essential ingredients in serene rooms. Think about the entertainment unit, something that blends in with its surroundings naturally and harmoniously.

Furniture upholstery is usually neutral toned and texturally rich: soft-to-the-touch tweeds, flannels, and herringbones—typical menswear fabrics—cotton, linen, and especially leather. Graphic, geometric patterns and boxy shapes are on pillows, with strong punches of gray, black, tan, and white.

It is perfectly fine in a serene room to leave the windows unadorned, and let the window itself speak as an architectural element. When you do need a window treatment, choose simple, light-enhancing, or diffusing shades, sheers, or blinds. Or, conversely, let the window treatment provide rich texture and color. In that case, choose strong monochromatic checks, stripes, or patterned fabrics. Nontraditional fabrics in the serene setting are theatrical scrim, burlap with threads pulled to create geometric patterns, raw silk, loosely woven netting, or paper.

Window hardware is equally simple. Hang fabric from brushed nickel or plain wooden or steel rods, wire, or industrial building materials such as copper or galvanized pipe.

Lighting should be unobtrusive or deliberately sculptural—glass, ceramic, woven grass, cork, or wood crafted into simple geometric, columnar, boxy, or slightly curved shapes.

Flooring should emphasize natural materials and solid craftsmanship. Floors could be inlaid, wide-plank, smooth or rich patina wood surfaces or glazed concrete, porcelain tile, slate, stone, or marble. Wall-to-wall carpet will be flat, solid color, or textured in tonal weaves such as a tweed or heathered wool. Jute or grass cloth with rougher textures, or a wool sisal for more tender feet, are neutral choices.

Accessories should be simple. Books, boxes, and framed pictures all offer square geometric shapes. Ceramics, baskets, and sculptural objects can be more shapely and curvaceous, visually breaking the strong vertical and horizontal lines of a room.

Walls in serene rooms take well to a simple paint job but also can be covered with grass cloth or raffia to complete the look.

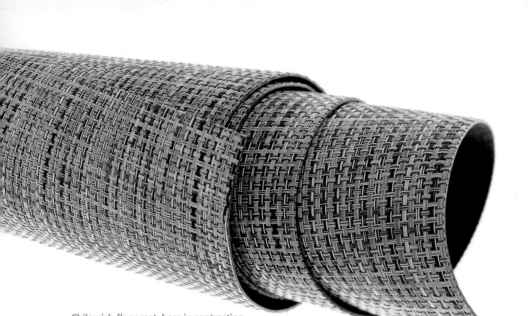

Chilewich floor mat, here in contrasting dark and light tones, provides a neutral layer in a serene space.

Abaca Irish Matting from A.M. Collections on the floor in Stephen Jacoby's living room provides a textural and tonal contrast to the check silk curtains from J. Robert Scott.

Our homes need to be serene *and* comfortable,

A grid of framed prints from a 1973 portfolio entitled, "The New York Collection for Stockholm," which includes works by Roy Lichtenstein and Donald Judd, hangs in the dining room of Stephen Jacoby.

Upholstery trim for serene style is straightforward and textural. Cotton and silk tape, cording, and tassels provide dressmaker detail without a lot of fuss.

A side table in Jacoby's living room from Palumbo 20th-Century Furniture combines a drawer with open shelf space and is the perfect spot to display a box, a Buddha, and a lamp.

A trio of hand-hammered lamps with shapes, patina, and texture that complement a serene setting—a large, antique-finished copper base with an ivory linen shade from McGuire, a silver sphere on a wrought-iron stand from Currey & Co., and a small brass lamp from Ikea.

Yards of simple white linen glide easily on wire hardware from Houles in Boston in this bedroom designed by Tinatin Kilaberidze in Vermont.

emotionally rich and sensually fulfilling.

At the home of Bob Sweet, a stone Buddha from Thailand sits outside on the deck in a spot designated for yoga and meditation.

A pyramid étagère in dark-finished maple offers clean lines and an elegant shape on which to display objects.

SENSORY BOX

Sight: Grass-cloth wall-covering, eggshell paints, ceramic collections

Scent: Rosemary, sage, sandlewood

Sound: Running water, classical guitar, birdsong

Taste: Green apples, green tea, bottled water

Touch: Chenille throw, polarfil pillow, sheer canopy

Botanicals from Longstreet Collection, created using a 19th-century process called photogram, depict ferns, leaves, and prairie grasses—nature framed for hanging.

In my living room I like to place an area rug over sisal, especially in the colder months, for a rich, layered look.

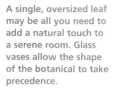

A single, oversized leaf may be all you need to add a natural touch to a serene room. Glass vases allow the shape of the botanical to take precedence.

Translucent, clean-lined, monochromatic,

Natural flooring essentials—woven grass cloth, wooden planks, slate tile, or linoleum fashioned to look like granite or stone.

Luxurious bed linens emphasize the tactile experience of plush down, crisp fabric with mitered corners, and soft folds over color and pattern.

A simple fabric pattern depicts a botanical rendering in neutral tones on this clean-lined, attached cushion upholstered chair with matching ottoman.

A chair, upholstered in a natural woven grass cloth, has added texture with a basketweave. A collection of ceramic vases varies the texture of the books and print on the shelf.

A black-and-white photograph on a beadboard wall provides a subtle touch of elegance in this clean, simple bedroom.

Dressmaker construction details—sharp corners and button trim—work in the serene style but are simpler and more understated.

or textural—essentials for Serene style.

A utilitarian, clean-lined, nickel-plated lamp with matching shade is the essence of a serene tablelight.

Fluted, rimmed, or smooth—collections may vary surface texture but keep with a monochromatic color scheme.

The graceful shape of a Lucite side chair on a white carpet with a silk-string curtain in back gives this vignette in the home of Bob Sweet an otherworldly, serene quality.

Simple matchstick blinds crafted from natural grasses offer privacy and act as a light filter while remaining part of a textural, neutral background.

Sunlight and shadow add drama to a collection of shapely vases on a side table in the home of Bill Cook in Atlanta.

Dark and light contrasts of black-and-white photography are repeated in the beaded pillow on the sofa in Cook's living room.

Serene materials include glass, ceramics,

A floating shelf and cleverly concealed lighting replace the more traditional side table and lamp next to this seating area, helping to avoid visual clutter while utilizing a wall to maximum advantage.

Variously shaped and hued vessels provide interesting form and color when displayed in a serene setting. Though each shape is unique, the repetition of their organic shapes holds the collection together.

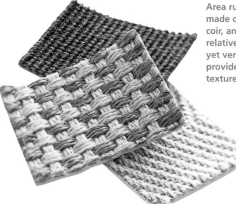

Area rugs and carpet made of jute, seagrass, coir, and sisal are relatively inexpensive yet very durable and provide an interesting texture underfoot.

A Lucite side table from Lobel Modern in Stephen Jacoby's New York City apartment supports a model airplane and aids in the illusion that the plane is actually in flight.

Squares, cylinders, and rectangles provide pleasing geometry to a collection of candles—essential ingredients in a serene setting. Glass vessels contain scented candles.

The clean-lined, boxy shape of a sage-colored upholstered, mid-century modern side chair provides seating and a display space for a stack of books.

wax, woven grasses, wood, metal, acrylic, and leather.

A wall/storage unit in the home of designer Bill Cook combines mid-century sensibilities with high technology. The black leather swivel egg chair is by Arne Jacobsen.

Monochromatic colors combined with varied textures such as wood, metal, sisal, wool, and vinyl trump pattern on this collection of stools.

Pattern, when it appears in the serene setting, is often in the form of stripes or contrasting blocks of toned-down color such as in this collection of woven natural materials.

resources

Designers & Architects

Warren and Mai Arthur
316 Grove Street
New Canaan, CT 06840
(203) 966-5528

Stephen Beili
Tierra Concepts
1807 Second Street, Suite 100
Santa Fe, NM 87505
(505) 989-8484

Belcaro Fine Arts
Kathleen Scheinfeld
455 Lorraine Blvd.
Los Angeles, CA 90020
(323) 525-1805

Merilee Bostock Interiors
7 Manursing Island
Rye, NY 10580
(914) 967-2056

Bill Cook
Vermilion Designs/ Interiors
1801 Friar Tuck Road, NE
Atlanta, GA 30309
(404) 874-4934

James D'Auria
20 West 36th Street, 12th Floor
New York, NY 10018
(212) 268-1142

Louise Drevenstam
LCD Interior Design, Inc.
Greenwich, CT 06830
(203) 661-6770

Judith Driscoll
1896 Walter Street
Maplewood, MN 55109
(651) 793-9495

Mark Finlay
1300 Post Road, Suite 101
Fairfield, CT 06430
(203) 254-2388

Toni Gallagher
10 Thistle Lane
Rye, NY 10580
(914) 967-7609

Gunkelmans Interior Design
R. Thomas Gunkelman
81 South 9th Street, Suite 340
Minneapolis, MN 55402
(612) 333-0526

Victoria Hagan Interiors
654 Madison Avenue
New York, NY 10021
(212) 888-1178

Tinatin Kilaberidze
Interior Design
PO Box 135
Calais, VT 05648
(802) 229-5621

Landmark Restoration
455 Lorraine Blvd.
Los Angeles, CA 90020
(323) 525-1805

Leess Design
Ingrid Bjelland Leess
228 Canoe Hill Road
New Canaan, CT 06840
(203) 972-0631

John T. Midyette III
and Associates, Architects
1125 Canyon Road
Santa Fe, NM 87501
(505) 983-2639

Stephen Miller Siegel
Brown Siegel Design Associates
595 Madison Avenue, Suite 1300
New York, NY 10022
(212) 832-5400

Stephanie Stokes
139 East 57th Street
New York, NY 10022
(212) 756-9922

Lynn von Kersting
Indigo Seas Co.
123 North Roberston Blvd.
Los Angeles, CA 90048

Furniture & Accessories

ABC Carpet & Home
888 Broadway
New York, NY 10021
(212) 988-5248

The Accessory Store
69 Jefferson Street
Stamford, CT 06902
(203) 327-7128
Lamps, shades, hardware

Aero Ltd.
132 Spring Street
New York, NY 10012
(212) 966-1500

Al Friedman
431 Boston Post Road
Port Chester, NY 10573
(914) 937-7351

Antan
28 East Putnam Avenue
Riverside, CT 06878
(203) 698-3219

Anthropologie
(800) 309-2500
www.anthropologie.com

Bankstreet Fabrics
115 New Canaan Avenue
Norwalk, CT 06850
(203) 846-1333

Bassett Furniture
PO Box 626
Bassett, VA 24055
(540) 629-6000
www.bassettfurniture.com

Braemore Textiles
Division of P. Kaufman, Inc.
2 Park Avenue
New York, NY 10016
(212) 292-3286

Carpet Trends, Inc.
5 Smith Street
Rye, NY 10580
(914) 967-5188

Catch Can II
5516 Connecticut Avenue, NW
Washington, DC 20015
(202) 686-5316

Chatsworth
Auction Rooms & Furniture Studios, Inc.
151 Mamaroneck Avenue
Mamaroneck, NY 10543
(914) 698-1001

Chris Upholstery
73 Main Street
Norwalk, CT 06851
(203) 849-7716

Clementine of Greenwich
85 Greenwich Avenue
Greenwich, CT 06830
(203) 869-9787

Connecticut Avenue Collection
John T. Atkins
5520 Connecticut Avenue, NW
Washington, DC 20015
(202) 243-0133

Crate & Barrel
(800) 996-9960
(800) 323-5461 (catalog)
www.crateandbarrel.com

Debbie's Stamford Antiques
  Center, Inc.
737 Canal Street
Stamford, CT 06902
(203) 357-0622

Farrow & Ball, Inc.
Uddens Estate
Wimborne
Dorset
BH21 7NL
United Kingdom
(845) 369-4912
www.farrow-ball.com

Steve Fisher
Stone Man Masonry
Grafton, VT
(802) 843-2282

Floral Fashions
502 Westchester Avenue
Port Chester, NY 10573
(914) 937-3871

Glenn Horowitz Booksellers
East Hampton, NY
(632) 324-5511

Homer
939 Madison Avenue
New York, NY 10021
(212) 744-7705
www.homerdesign.com

IKEA
www.ikea-usa.com

Indigo Seas
123 North Robertson Blvd.
Los Angeles, CA 90048
(310) 550-8758

JC Penney Home
One Lincoln Center, 14th Floor
PO Box 10001
Dallas, TX 75301
(800) 222-6161
www.jcpenney.com

Jonathan Adler
New York, NY
(212) 941-8950

Keleen Leathers
Westchester, IL
(708) 409-9800

The Kellogg Collection, Inc.
3424 Wisconsin Avenue, NW
Washington, DC 20016-3009

Lark Upson Design
(802) 476-8003
Custom furniture

Lillian August Warehouse
85 Water Street
South Norwalk, CT 06854
(203) 838-0153

Lobel Modern
New York, NY
(212) 242-9075

Mabley-Handler Home Store
30 East Putnam Avenue
Greenwich, CT 06830
(203) 618-1761

McHugh Antiques
Cooper Avenue
Aspen, CO 81612

Nicole Keane
N. Keen & Co.
4181 Historic Route 7A,
PO Box 24
Manchester Village, VT 05254
(802) 362-9950

Palumbo 20th Century
Furniture & Objects
New York, NY
(212) 734-7630

Pottery Barn
(800) 922-5507
www.potterybarn.com

Restoration Hardware
(800) 762-1005
www.restorationhardware.com

Rogers & Goffigon, Ltd.
41 Chestnut Street
Greenwich, CT 06830
(203) 532-8068

F. Schumacher & Co.
79 Madison Avenue
New York, NY 10016
(212) 213-7900
www.fschumacher.com

Seabrook Wallcoverings
1325 Farmville Road
Memphis, TN 38122
(800) 238-9152
www.seabrookwallcoverings.com

The Silk Trading Company
888 Broadway
New York, NY 10003
(212) 966-5464
www.silktrading.com

Smith & Noble
1181 California Avenue
Corona, CA 92881
(909) 734 444
www.smithandnoble.com

Simon Pearce Glass
Windsor Industrial Park
Windsor, VT 05089
(802) 674-6280
www.SimonPearce.com

Taos Furniture
Keith Gorges
(505) 780-1152

Weathervane Hill
Company Store
Loehmann's Plaza
467 West Avenue
Norwalk, CT 06850
(203) 838-2999

Woodard & Greenstein
Woodard Weave
Classic American Woven Rugs
506 East 74th Street, Fifth Floor
New York, NY 10021
(212) 988-2906

index

photography credits

All photographs are by Nancy E. Hill except the following:

Cover: Daniela Stallinger

Jonelle Weaver, pages 36-39

Edward Addeo, pages 58-63, 104-105, 150-155

Antonis Achillios, pages 27, 57-63, 73, 103-109, 119, 149, 150-155

Miki Duisterhof, page 21

Jennifer Lévy, pages 22, 23, 32, 33, 60, 68, 69, 71, 87, 89, 108, 114, 115, 152, 154

notes